Our Heritage Continues...

Into the 21st Century

Order Sons of Italy in America
Grand Lodge of Florida

Our second cookbook, *Our Italian Heritage Continues…Into the 21st Century*, is the latest compilation of traditional family recipes from local lodge members in the Grand Lodge of Florida.

Proceeds from the sale of this book will be used by the Grand Lodge of Florida to support the initiatives set out in its Constitution.

Our first cookbook, *Preserving Our Italian Heritage*, placed second in the 1991 National TABASCO Community Awards Cookbook competition. The award was presented by Paul C.P. McIlhenny, Vice President of the McIlhenny Company, before the annual conference of The American Institute of Wine and Food in New Orleans, Louisiana.

You enjoyed our first cookbook…you will love our sequel.

Additional copies may be obtained from Grand Lodge of Florida website: **www.osiafl.org** or by contacting:

> Dennis Piasio
>
> Grand Lodge of Florida
>
> 5187 Woodstone Circle E.
>
> Lake Worth, FL 33463
>
> (561) 641-1643

TABLE OF CONTENTS

From the President 5

Acknowledgment 6

Antipasti (Appetizers) 7

Minestre (Soup) 23

Pane e Pizze (Bread and Pizza) 39

Le Uova (Eggs) 47

Salsa-Pasta-Riso-Polenta (Sauce-Pasta-Rice-Polenta) 53

Carne-Pollo-Pesce (Meat-Chicken-Fish) 83

Insalate e Contorni (Salads and Vegetables) 133

Dolci e Feste (Desserts and Holiday Recipes) 159

Index 209

From the Past President

It is with great pride that I introduce to you our second cookbook which maintains the tried and true traditions of Italian culinary expertise, as handed down from generation to generation.

This cookbook is a compilation of various regions of Italy that exemplifies traditions, skills and pride. The Daughters and Sons of Italy have risen to the challenge of bringing another exceptional edition to the world of food preparation for all to experience by meeting the highest standards of cooking the Italian way.

Unlike many cookbooks, our members in the Sons of Italy, Grand Lodge of Florida, have provided traditional recipes to preserve the richness and history of Italy. Authenticity has been the rule for every member to adhere to.

Also, Italian taste and technique have been basic cooking elements as far back as the Renaissance period. Italian technique is knowing how to prepare ingredients in the finest possible manner. This has been handed down through generations and continues today.

As you review these pages, you will certainly be inspired to put many of these home-styled recipes on your dinner table. You will get the same results as nonna, who made dinner so tasteful from her pieces of paper, sometimes scribbled in Italian, with signs of her sauce or gravy on it.

Cooking is a language all its own, and you are now ready to enter the exciting world of Italian cuisine. Join us in becoming tomorrow's 'nonna'.

Enjoy and Buon Appetito!

Dennis J. Piasio

From the President

Many of you have enjoyed using the recipes of our members in our first cookbook, *Preserving Our Italian Heritage*. Now you are going to enjoy a new selection of recipes in our second cookbook, *Our Heritage Continues . . . Into the 21st Century*.

If this is your first visit into our Order Sons of Italy, Grand Lodge of Florida recipe selections, you're in for a treat. These traditional recipes passed down from generation to generation from our Italian families will surely become family favorites in your home.

In Cookbook II, you will see recipes from many of the regions throughout Italy. You'll find recipes from Antipasti to Dolci. Just add a little wine to your dinner and anisette for your demitasse, and you have a meal that will be better than most Italian restaurants in your neighborhood. In most restaurants you leave full, at your dinner table family and friends will leave full and fulfilled.

In the Italian tradition, the cook expresses their love for their guests through the food they prepare. In cookbook II you will find many ways to express your love for your guests.

I want to thank the members of the Order Sons of Italy, Grand Lodge of Florida who submitted their family recipes for this second edition. We certainly enjoyed putting this edition together for you.

Lastly, special thanks go out to Cheryl Mauro Berg for her personal effort in making this cookbook a reality.

Enjoy and Buon Appetito!

Dan Cositore, State President

Order Sons of Italy

Grand Lodge of Florida

Editor's Note

Our Florida filial lodge members have again come forward with new recipes for the latest compilation of our state's cookbook.

These recipes have been gleaned from well-kept family files. Our ancestors came from all over Italy, most speaking their regional dialect. We were raised hearing the names of our favorite dishes in dialect. Recipes that were hand-written were done so with names and ingredients written as they were spoken. We have translated these recipes from dialect to Italian, but when uncertain, we left the name or ingredient as submitted.

On occasion, we included recipes when either the contributor's name and/or lodge was missing. The recipes were too good to leave out! We also included recipes that had ingredient quantities missing, if we felt the recipe had enough merit to include in this book. You will need to draw comparisons from recipes that are similar, perhaps even drawing quantities from your own family files. Or do as many terrific Italian cooks do in the home - *experiment*, but don't forget to enter your adjustments on the page.

One feature of this book is the inclusion of blank pages at the end of each section. These pages have been set aside so that you may include *your* favorite Italian recipes from family and friends.

Committee:	Cheryl Mauro Berg	editor
	Joneanne Venable	assistant editor
	Kristin Berengolts	data entry
	Dennis Berg	data entry
	Maria Kendrick	proofreader
	Caterina Lionti	graphic designer

Preparation and Cooking Tips:

- Read the recipe in its entirety, so that you may prepare ingredients ahead of time.
- When you see **salt, salt / pepper, pepper, or red pepper flakes**, you will add these ingredients to your taste.
- Bring your pasta water to a boil while you are preparing other ingredients, unless otherwise specified. Salt the water immediately before or after adding pasta to the boiling water.
- Bread flour refers to King Arthur Unbleached Bread Flour.

Antipasti

La Nuova Sicilia Lodge 1251
Tampa

Lake Worth-Boynton Beach Lodge 2304
Lake Worth

Dominick Gentile Lodge 2332
Coral Springs - Margate

Stuart Lodge 2337
Stuart

Joseph B. Franzalia Lodge 2422
Ft. Walton Beach

Antipasti

Artichoke Dip

1 cup grated parmesan cheese
1 cup mayonnaise

1 (14 oz.) jar artichoke hearts, drained
garlic powder

Mix all ingredients thoroughly in blender. Serve hot or cold with crackers or chips. May be served hot by heating in the oven until just hot. Serves 8 to 10.

Jean D'Antonio Fineberg
John Paul I Lodge #2427

Artichoke Hearts

2 (14 oz.) cans artichoke hearts
4 tbsp. olive oil
2 tbsp. lemon juice

1/2 tsp. oregano
salt / pepper
1 tbsp. capers, chopped
lettuce

Drain artichoke hearts and place in a bowl. Combine oil, lemon juice, oregano, salt and pepper to taste. Pour over artichoke hearts. Allow to marinate for several hours, stirring occasionally. Serve on lettuce and sprinkle with chopped capers. Serves 6.

Margaret Scarfia
John Paul I Lodge #2427

Garlic Crostini

1 loaf Italian bread
1 clove garlic, halved

virgin olive oil

Heat oven to 375 degrees. Slice bread into 3/4 inch slices. Brush lightly with olive oil on both sides. Place slices on a baking sheet. Bake each side until golden brown. While bread is still warm, rub garlic on the crostini. Cool. Store in a tin.

Irene Lamano
St. Cloud/Kissimmee Lodge #2731

Antipasti

Antipasto

My dad always made this before dinner on every holiday, with so much joy and pride. We always looked forward to his antipasto. I hope you enjoy this dish as much as we did.

1 jar pickled eggplant, with juice
1 jar pickled small onions
1 jar roasted peppers, with juice
1 jar giardiniera
green and black olives
1 red onion, sliced
celery, sliced
radishes, cut in quarters
1 jar pickled peppers, cut in halves
1 can cut string beans
1 can chickpeas
1 can straw mushrooms or fresh mushrooms, halved
2 cans artichoke hearts
Genoa salami slices
provolone cheese slices
olive oil

In a large bowl or pan mix everything together, except the salami and provolone cheese. On a serving platter, place the salami and cheese slices around the edge of the plate and put the mixed ingredients in the center; add some radishes made into flowers for decoration. Serve with Italian bread and enjoy.

Ralph Natrillo
father of Angela Harrington
Dominick Gentile Lodge #2332

Antipasti

Bagno Caldo alla Siciliana
Hot Dip Italian Style

1/4 cup olive oil
3 cloves garlic, minced
2 green onions (bulb only), minced
salt / pepper

2 oz. anchovies
1/2 tsp. Tabasco sauce
4 tbsp. wine vinegar
2 tsp. roasted pimiento, chopped
vegetables for dipping

In a medium-size skillet heat olive oil and simmer garlic, onions, salt and pepper for 5 minutes. Add anchovies and blend with a fork. Add Tabasco sauce, wine vinegar and roasted pimiento and mix well. Simmer slowly. Pour sauce into a chafing dish to keep warm. Use freshly washed vegetables that can be eaten raw.

Margaret Scarfia
John Paul I Lodge #2427

Bruschetta

2 cups chopped ripe tomatoes
   or 15 oz. can tomatoes
1/2 red onion, diced
2 tbsp. chopped fresh basil
2 garlic cloves, minced
1 tsp. capers, coarsely chopped
1 tbsp. extra virgin olive oil
1 tsp. balsamic vinegar

1 loaf Italian bread, sliced
   1 to 1 ½ inch thick
2 garlic cloves, halved
extra virgin olive oil, to serve
fresh mozzarella, 1/4 inch slices
whole capers and whole basil
   leaves, for garnish

Combine first 7 ingredients in a medium bowl; cover and refrigerate. Place slices of Italian bread under the broiler; brown the tops only. Remove bread from the broiler and rub the toasted top of each slice with the garlic. Drizzle with a little olive oil. Spoon some of the tomato mixture on top of each slice and crown with the fresh mozzarella. Serve 2 to 3 slices on a plate as an appetizer. Garnish with a few whole capers and whole basil leaves.

Ann DeMarco
John Paul I Lodge #2427

Antipasti

Bruschetta with Tomatoes

3 to 4 tomatoes, chopped
salt / pepper, ground fresh
a few leaves fresh basil, chopped

8 slices crusty white bread
2 to 3 cloves garlic
6 tbsp. olive oil

Place chopped tomatoes with juice in a small bowl. Season with salt and pepper and stir in basil. Let stand for 10 minutes. Toast or broil bread on both sides until crisp. Rub one side with garlic. Arrange on a platter. Sprinkle with olive oil. Spoon tomatoes on top and serve at once. Serves 4.

Barbara Hoff
Plano, Texas

BLT Bites

16 to 20 cherry tomatoes
1 lb. bacon, cooked
  and crumbled
1/2 cup mayonnaise
  or salad dressing

1/3 cup chopped green onions
3 tbsp. grated parmesan cheese
2 tbsp. snipped fresh parsley

Cut a thin slice off each tomato top. Scoop out and discard pulp. Invert tomato on a paper towel to drain. In a small bowl, combine the remaining ingredients. Mix well. Spoon into tomatoes. Refrigerate for several hours.

Eleanor Santore
Port Charlotte Lodge #2507

Antipasti

Cheesy Italian Bread

2 tbsp. oil
3 garlic cloves, chopped
6 medium tomatoes,
    peeled and diced
1 tbsp. oregano

salt / pepper
8 large slices Italian bread,
    toasted
1/2 cup grated mozzarella

Preheat oven to 375 degrees. Heat oil in frying pan. When hot add garlic, tomatoes and oregano; season well and cook 10 minutes. Arrange bread on cookie sheet and top with tomato mixture. Cover with cheese. Change oven setting to broil and cook until cheese is melted and bubbly.

Tanya "Toni" Little
Frisco, Texas

Crocchette
Croquettes

1 cup bread crumbs
4 extra large eggs, beaten
1/2 cup parmesan cheese,
    freshly grated
2 tbsp. chopped parsley
2 tbsp. minced onion

1 pinch of nutmeg
1/2 tsp. salt
freshly ground black pepper
1/3 cup milk
1/2 cup light oil

Combine all ingredients except milk and oil in a bowl and mix thoroughly. Add milk a little at a time, stirring constantly until dough is formed. This can be made ahead of time up to this point. Heat oil for frying. Scoop batter with a tablespoon, and using a teaspoon, slide batter into oil. Cook until golden on all sides and drain on paper towels. Be careful not to crowd them. Keep warm until all are cooked. Serve as an appetizer with lemon wedges or with a light tomato sauce for a side dish in place of potatoes or pasta.

Therese Quattrochi Simpson
Bradenton Lodge #2782

Antipasti

Clam Dip

This is a favorite in the Cositore home. It's like eating baked clams without the shells.

2 (8 oz.) cans minced clams
1 tbsp. lemon juice
1/4 lb. butter
1/2 large chopped onion
5 cloves minced garlic
1 tsp. parsley flakes

1 tsp. oregano
3 to 4 dashes Tabasco sauce
salt / 5 shakes pepper
bread crumbs
parmesan cheese

In a small saucepan simmer clams with liquid and lemon juice for 15 minutes. In a separate frying pan, melt butter and sauté onion, garlic, parsley, oregano, Tabasco sauce, salt and pepper for 5 minutes. Blend both mixtures and 1/2 cup bread crumbs. Sprinkle with parmesan cheese and bake at 400 degrees for 20 minutes. If serving later, bake for 10 minutes, then 20 minutes just before serving. Serve with triscuits.

Dan Cositore
Societa d'Italia Lodge #2698

Crusty Italian Sausage Bites

1 tbsp. olive oil
1 onion, chopped
1 clove garlic, chopped
3/4 lb. Italian sausage, sliced
1 (14 oz.) can tomato sauce

salt / pepper
1 loaf French bread,
    sliced 1 inch thick, toasted
1 cup mozzarella cheese,
    grated

Heat oil in a skillet over medium heat. Add the onion and garlic. Sauté for 4 minutes. Add the sausage slices. Brown well and cook for 7 to 8 minutes. Pour in the tomato sauce. Simmer 6 to 8 minutes. Add salt and pepper to taste. Place the mixture into the bowl of a food processor and blend. Spread over toasted bread and place on an oven-proof platter. Top with mozzarella cheese. Broil in the oven until bubbly.

Pauline Parker
Ft. Walton Beach Lodge #2422

Eggplant Sandwiches

2 medium eggplants,
    cut into 1/4 inch thick slices
olive oil

20 fresh basil leaves
1/2 lb. provolone, thinly sliced
1/4 lb. prosciutto, thinly sliced

Preheat oven to 450 degrees. Lightly brush 2 flat pans with olive oil. Arrange the eggplant slices in a single layer on the pans. Bake for 20 minutes, turning once; eggplant should take on some color. Remove trays from the oven. Place one leaf of basil on half the eggplant slices. Top basil with provolone and prosciutto that has been cut to fit the eggplant slices. Place remaining eggplant in layers to form a sandwich. Brush tops with olive oil. Return to the oven and bake for 5 minutes or until cheese melts. Serves 6.

Pauline Parker
Ft. Walton Beach Lodge #2422

Insalata con Olive
Olive Salad

1/4 lb. green Italian olives, pitted
1/4 lb. black Italian olives, pitted
5 pickled green peppers,
    cut in eighths
1/4 cup olive oil

1/2 cup celery, diced
1 large onion, sliced
1 tbsp. oregano
salt / pepper
1/4 cup wine vinegar

Combine all ingredients and mix well. This may be used as an antipasto, salad or condiment with fish or pork. Keeps well in the refrigerator.

Ann DeMarco
John Paul I Lodge #2427

Antipasti

Grilled Warm Antipasto

1 medium eggplant
1 medium zucchini
1 yellow onion
1 large red pepper
1 large green pepper
1 large yellow pepper
3 large portabella mushrooms

olive oil
salt / pepper
garlic powder
3 tbsp. balsamic vinegar
1 tbsp. minced parsley
1 tsp. dried oregano

Slice cleaned vegetables into 1/2 inch thick slices. Brush vegetables with olive oil, season with salt and pepper. Sprinkle with garlic powder. Place vegetables on a hot grill and cook until tender. Place on a large platter, drizzle with vinegar and top with herbs. Serve warm or at room temperature.

Pauline Parker
Ft. Walton Beach Lodge #2422

Lumache Marchigiana

1 lb. live snails
1 tbsp. salt, repeated
1 tbsp. vinegar, repeated
4 tbsp. olive oil
1/4 cup chopped onion
2 cloves garlic, minced

1 cup white wine
2 tbsp. tomato paste, diluted
   with 1/2 cup water
1/2 tsp. thyme
salt / pepper

Place snails in a large container of cold water with the salt and vinegar. Stir with hands. Continue changing water, adding salt and vinegar each time, until the water is clear.

Place snails in a pan and cover with cold water. Bring to a boil and cook for 10 minutes, skimming foam from the top. Drain and cool.

Sauté the onion and garlic in the olive oil. Add wine and snails. Simmer for 20 minutes, then add tomato paste, thyme, and salt and pepper to taste. Simmer another 20 minutes. Serve hot with toasted bread. Enjoy.

Margaret Scarfia
John Paul I Lodge #2427

Antipasti

Fiori di Zucchini Fritti
Fried Zucchini Flowers

24 zucchini flowers
6 heaping tbsp. flour
1 pinch of salt
1 can of beer
6 cups vegetable oil

Do not wash the flowers. Clean carefully with a damp cloth. Completely remove the pistils. Combine the flour and salt in a deep bowl. Blend in the beer and mix until a smooth batter forms. Set aside. Heat oil to boiling in a deep frying pan. Dip each flower into the batter and immediately drop into the oil. Fry flowers until golden brown. Drain on paper towels. Sprinkle with salt. Serve hot. Serves 4.

Pauline Parker
Ft. Walton Beach Lodge #2422

Pepperoni Stuffed Mushrooms

24 large mushrooms
2 tbsp. olive oil
1/4 cup finely chopped onion
2 tbsp. chopped green or
    red sweet peppers
1 clove garlic, minced
1/2 tsp. dried oregano or basil
1/3 cup pepperoni, finely
    chopped
2 tbsp. bread crumbs

Wash and dry mushrooms. Remove and chop stems, which should equal approximately 2 cups. Set aside the caps.

Heat the olive oil in large skillet. Add the chopped stems, onion, peppers, garlic and oregano until tender; about 5 minutes. Stir as needed. Remove from heat, stir in pepperoni and bread crumbs.

Spoon 1 tablespoon of mixture in each reserved mushroom cap. Press lightly. Arrange mushrooms on a 15x10x1 inch baking sheet. Bake uncovered at 450 degrees for 8 to 10 minutes or until mushrooms are heated through. Serve warm.

Paulette Lombino
Ontario, NY

Antipasti

Mozzarella Croquettes

1/2 lb. mozzarella
3/4 cup flour
1 egg

1 tsp. salt
1 cup olive oil

Squeeze mozzarella in bowl until it becomes soft (fresh mozzarella works best). Add 1 tablespoon flour, egg and salt. Mix well. Make small shapes of croquettes and roll in the remaining flour. Place in hot oil and fry to a nice golden brown.

Dennis Piasio
Lake Worth/Boynton Beach Lodge #2304

Mushrooms in Vinegar

1/2 lb. button mushrooms
1 tbsp. whole mixed spices
1 clove garlic

1 tsp. salt
1 1/2 cups wine vinegar
1/4 cup oil

Wipe mushrooms with damp cloth. Heat vinegar until warm. Mix spices, garlic and salt. Put mushrooms in a sterilized jar. Pour vinegar mixture over and stir well. Cover jar tightly and allow to stand about 2 days. Add oil before serving. Serves 4.

Margaret Scarfia
John Paul I Lodge #2427

Sausage Cheese Balls

1 lb. extra sharp cheddar, grated
1 1/2 lbs. hot sausage,
    removed from casings

3 cups Bisquick

Mix all ingredients together. Knead and shape into little balls. Bake at 350 degrees for 20 minutes. *Note*: Recipe can be frozen.

Mary Ann Rawdon
St. Augustine Lodge #2780

Antipasti

Ricotta and Tomato Bruschetta

8 oz. loaf Italian bread
8 oz. ricotta cheese
   (whole or part skim)
1 tsp. minced fresh oregano leaves
1/4 tsp. ground black pepper
2 ripe medium tomatoes,
   seeded and diced

1/4 tsp. salt
3 tbsp. olive oil, separated
2 tsp. minced fresh parsley
   leaves, separated
2 cloves garlic, cut in half

Prepare outdoor grill. Cut off ends from loaf of bread; slice loaf diagonally into 1/2 inch thick slices. In a small bowl, mix together the cheese, oregano and pepper. In a medium bowl, stir together tomatoes, salt, 2 tablespoons olive oil and 1 teaspoon parsley. Place bread slices on grill over medium heat for 3 to 5 minutes on each side until lightly toasted. Rub 1 side of each piece of toast with garlic. Brush with remaining olive oil. Just before serving, spread ricotta cheese mixture on toast and top with tomato mixture. Sprinkle with remaining parsley.

Irene Lamano
St. Cloud/Kissimmee Lodge #2731

Tomatoes, Mozzarella, Anchovy and Black Olives

2 medium tomatoes
1/2 lb. mozzarella
1 can anchovy fillets
1 tbsp. capers

lemon juice
   or Italian dressing
black olives for garnish

Slice tomatoes and mozzarella. Place in a serving dish, alternating mozzarella and tomatoes. Place anchovies on top with a sprinkle of capers, and lemon juice or Italian dressing. Black olives optional.

Margaret Scarfia
John Paul I Lodge #2427

Antipasti

Tuna with Onion

1 large can tuna
pepper
1 tbsp. capers (optional)

1 onion, chopped
1 tbsp. chopped parsley
2 tbsp. lemon juice

Drain tuna. Break up tuna and place on a serving dish. Sprinkle with pepper, capers, chopped onion and parsley. Sprinkle lemon juice over tuna and serve.

Margaret Scarfia
John Paul I Lodge #2427

Imbattite di Memy
Stuffed Anchovy Appetizer

Origin: My cousin, Memy Caponari DeRosa, Salerno, Italy.

16 fresh anchovies or small
    sardines
16 half strips mozzarella cheese
flour

salt / pepper
2 eggs, beaten
seasoned bread crumbs
olive oil

Wash anchovies. Remove spine carefully, do not split. Pat dry well. Stuff each cleaned anchovy with a mozzarella strip. Close tightly to make a sandwich. Roll in flour seasoned with salt and pepper. Dip in beaten egg and cover with seasoned bread crumbs. Fry quickly in hot olive oil until crispy light brown. Serve hot as an appetizer.

Rose Marie Boniello
Sgt. F. M. Bonnano Lodge #2549

Zucchini Quiche

3 cups grated zucchini
  (drained)
1 cup Bisquick
1/2 cup chopped onion
1/2 cup parmesan cheese
2 tbsp. parsley

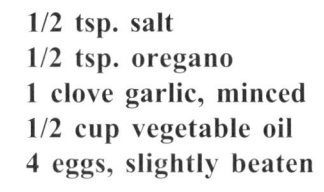

1/2 tsp. salt
1/2 tsp. oregano
1 clove garlic, minced
1/2 cup vegetable oil
4 eggs, slightly beaten

Heat oven to 350 degrees. Grease a 13 x 9 x 2 inch oblong pan. Mix all ingredients together; spread in the pan. Bake until golden brown, about 25 minutes.

Mary Ann Rawdon
St. Augustine Lodge #2780

Zucchini Pie

3 cups zucchini,
  sliced thin and diced
1 small onion, chopped
1 cup Bisquick
4 eggs

1/2 cup oil
1/2 cup parmesan cheese
1 tsp. parsley flakes
salt / pepper

Mix all ingredients together and pour into a baking dish. Bake at 350 degrees for 30 minutes or until golden brown. Cut into small squares and serve.

Jean D'Antonio Fineberg
John Paul I Lodge #2427

Antipasti

Personal Recipes:

Minestre

John Paul I Lodge 2427
St. Petersburg

John Rapisardi Lodge 2436
Key West

Mike Accardi Lodge 2441
Deltona

Orlando Lodge 2463
Orlando

Nature Coast Lodge 2502
Spring Hill

Minestre

Beef Soup

1 1/2 lbs. beef chuck or brisket
1 lb. beef soup bone with marrow
1 large can tomatoes
2 whole large carrots
1 large onion, quartered
2 sprigs parsley
2 celery stalks with leaves, halved
salt / pepper
1/2 lb. pastina

Place meat and bone in a soup kettle and cover with cold water. Bring slowly to a boil. Skim top with a spoon. Add all vegetables to the meat. Season with salt and pepper. Cover kettle and cook slowly over low heat until meat is done, about 2 hours. Remove meat and vegetables from soup and strain broth through a colander. Return soup to stove, add pastina and cook slowly 8 to 12 minutes until tender. Serve sprinkled with grated parmesan cheese, if desired.

Notes: The meat may be cut up and cooked in the soup with the pastina. The pastina may be cooked separately in 2 quarts boiling salted water and added to soup after it is done. This will result in a thinner soup.

Variations: If a spicy soup is desired, add 1/2 teaspoon whole mixed spices in the last hour of cooking. Remove the spices when the pastina is cooked.
Add bay leaf, if desired, when vegetables are added and remove it about 1 hour before soup is done.
One cup uncooked rice may be used in place of pastina. Cook it in the strained soup about 18 minutes, until a kernel crushes easily between thumb and finger.

Ann DeMarco
John Paul 1 Lodge #2427

Minestre

Bronx Home Run Zucchini Soup

Mom used to pick the squash from our garden during the summer months and tell us how much better our squash was than what you bought in the store ... and we saved money, too.

1 cup chopped onion
1/2 cup butter, salted
3 cups chicken broth
2 cups finely chopped zucchini
1 tsp. dried basil

1/2 tsp. salt
1/2 tsp. nutmeg
1/4 tsp. pepper
2 sprigs parsley, finely chopped

Sauté onion in butter until tender. Pour broth into a saucepan, add zucchini and bring to a boil. Lower heat and cover for 20 minutes. Mix in basil, salt, nutmeg and pepper. Serve hot with parsley garnish.

Dennis Piasio
Lake Worth/Boynton Beach Lodge #2304

Brown Rice and Lentil Soup

1 1/2 cups diced carrots
1 cup chopped onion
1/2 cup chopped celery
3 cloves garlic, chopped
1 (14 oz.) can tomatoes,
    coarsely chopped
8 cups chicken or vegetable stock
1 1/2 cups lentils

1 cup uncooked brown rice
1 1/2 tsp. dried basil
1 1/2 tsp. dried thyme
1 1/2 tsp. dried oregano
1/2 tsp. dried red pepper flakes
2 bay leaves
salt / pepper
parsley, chopped

In a large kettle combine all ingredients except parsley, salt and pepper. Bring to a boil, then reduce heat and simmer, stirring occasionally for about 35 minutes. Remove the bay leaves and season with salt and pepper. Add the parsley and serve. *Note:* The lentils do not need to be soaked before cooking.

Dolly Flaver
Rome, NY

Minestre

Ceci Soup

1/2 cup olive oil
1 clove garlic, finely chopped
1/2 tsp. rosemary
3 chopped anchovy fillets
1 tbsp. tomato paste

1/2 cup water
1 can chickpeas
1 cup elbow macaroni
1/2 tsp. salt
1/2 tsp. pepper

In a soup pot place olive oil, garlic, rosemary and anchovies. Heat to brown. Mix tomato paste and water and add to the soup pot. Cook for 1/2 hour over low flame. Add chickpeas, then fill the empty can with water and add to the pot. Bring to a boil, add salt and macaroni, and cook for 8 to 10 minutes. Add pepper and serve.

Dennis Piasio
Lake Worth/Boynton Beach Lodge #2304

Zuppa di Pollo
Chicken Soup

1 chicken, about 3 to 4 pounds
2 celery stalks with leaves, halved
2 sprigs parsley

2 peeled carrots
1 large ripe tomato (optional)
salt / pepper

Wash chicken thoroughly and place in a soup kettle. Add enough water to cover. Bring slowly to a boil. Skim surface. Add washed vegetables and seasonings to the pot. Cover tightly and cook slowly until the chicken is tender, about 2 1/2 hours. Strain broth, season and serve as desired.

Variations: Add 2 cups cooked rice to strained broth and heat until rice is hot; stir and serve.
Cook 1/2 pound pastina in 2 quarts boiling water, drain. Add to strained broth and chicken broken into small pieces; heat thoroughly.

Ann DeMarco
John Paul 1 Lodge #2427

Minestre

Chicken Soup

She grabs my hand and off we go...the most wonderful person my heart has touched until today - my grandmother. *Whatever she cooked, you ate. Why? She did it with such love. Even her fresh chicken soup ... as we neared the chicken market I could hear them, tears filled my eyes because I knew soon one of them would be our dinner. Talk about fresh chicken. Till this day I could not duplicate Grandma's soup. Maybe it was the suspense and fear that led up to the actual dinner.*

1 fresh chicken
1/2 lb. chopped meat
2 tbsp. grated cheese
2 tbsp. parsley
1 clove garlic
1/2 cup bread crumbs
1 egg
salt / pepper

3 carrots
3 potatoes
3 fresh fennel, stems only
1/4 bunch celery stalks
1 tomato
1/2 head escarole
1 onion
acini de pepe pasta

Soak chicken in salted water – do not remove feet (this is the tasty part of the chicken). Cut chicken into sections.

In a bowl, mix chopped meat with grated cheese, parsley, garlic, bread crumbs, egg, and salt and pepper to taste. The texture should be firm enough to make very small meat balls. If too firm, add a bit of water at a time until consistency changes. Place in a pot of water with chicken. Bring to a boil. Skim off foam. Lower heat. Cook 1/2 hour, then and add vegetables cut to preferred size. Add salt and pepper to taste. Leave onion whole and place in water. Cook for at least 1 1/2 hours on medium-low heat.

When soup is finished, boil water for pasta. Add a half cup of pasta for every four persons. Cook pasta 4 to 7 minutes. Drain the water and add pasta to soup.

Joanna Colonna
Osceola County Lodge #2523

Cioppino

1 lb. fish fillets
1 cup chopped onion
2 tsp. chopped garlic
1 (8 oz.) can tomato sauce
1 (28 oz.) can tomatoes, cut up
    or
6 fresh tomatoes, diced
1/2 cup white wine or chicken broth
1 tsp. dried basil
1 tsp. dried thyme
1 tsp. dried marjoram
1 tsp. dried oregano
1/4 tsp. pepper
1 tbsp. dried parsley flakes
1 bay leaf

In a saucepan, mix all ingredients, except fish. Simmer for 20 to 30 minutes, stirring occasionally. Meanwhile, cut fish into 1/2 inch chunks. Add fish to the saucepan and cook for 10 minutes or until done. Yield: 4 servings
Note: Fresh herbs are preferred, if available.

Irene Lamano
St. Cloud/Kissimmee Lodge #2731

Escarole, Bean, and Sausage Soup

2 tbsp. olive oil
3/4 lb. Italian sausage, diced
4 large garlic cloves, chopped
1 large head escarole,
    coarsely chopped
3 (14 oz.) cans chicken broth
1 (15 oz.) can cannellini beans
salt / pepper
parmesan cheese

Heat oil in a large dutch oven over medium heat. Add sausage and garlic and sauté until sausage is lightly brown for about 8 minutes. Add escarole and cook until tender. Add broth and cannellini beans with their juice. Simmer until flavor blends and soup thickens for about 20 minutes. Season to taste with salt and pepper. Serve with parmesan cheese.

Pauline Parker
Ft. Walton Beach Lodge #2422

Minestre

Joey's White Bean and Sausage Soup

This is an original from my son, Joseph Cuzzolina. My father, Joseph Agnetti, was a butcher and chef by trade. Apparently, the chef genes must skip a generation because I didn't get them.

1 lb. bag small white or Navy beans	1 large yellow onion, chopped
2 tbsp. dried basil	olive oil
1 tbsp. dried oregano	1 large red pepper, chopped
2 tbsp. minced garlic	1 lb. mushrooms, sliced
1 pkg. spicy Italian sausage	salt / pepper

Put beans in a large pot with 2 quarts of water; soak overnight.

Drain beans and rinse. Place the beans back in the pot with about 3 quarts of water. Place on burner set to high. Add all of the seasonsings and garlic to the water. Do not put a lid on the pot.

Remove the casings from the sausage. Sauté and chop the sausage into small bite-size pieces in the pan until fully cooked. Empty the contents of the pan (including the oil or grease for flavor) into the pot which should be at a boil. Stir the soup every 5 minutes until done, being sure to scrape the spoon on the bottom of the pot to remove any beans that begin to stick.

In the same pan sauté the onions with about 2 tablespoons of olive oil until cooked (not slimy), and add to the pot. Repeat with the red pepper. Repeat with the mushrooms but add a little salt and pepper to the mushrooms (and a little red wine). By now you're probably wondering if you can turn the burner down, because the soup is splashing all over the place and the pot is pretty full. NO. The hard boil you have going is necessary to break down the beans and needs to be maintained. Stir the soup frequently for the remainder of the cooking time. If the soup starts to get too thick, add some water (a cup or two will usually do). Soup mixture should cook about 30 minutes.

You'll know the soup is done when its consistency approaches that of a stew and it is tannish in color. If it seems too thick or thin, either add water or cook it longer. You can garnish with some thinly sliced scallions.

Louise Agnetti
Societa d'Italia Lodge #2698

Mediterranean Chickpea, Tomato, and Pasta Soup

2 tbsp. olive oil
1 cup onion, diced
1 1/3 cup water
1 (16 oz.) can chicken broth
1 (15 oz.) can chickpeas, drained
1 (14 oz.) can diced tomatoes, undrained
1/2 tsp. cumin
1/2 tsp. cinnamon
1/4 tsp. black pepper
1/2 cup uncooked ditalini
2 tbsp. chopped fresh parsley

In a soup pot, sauté onion in olive oil until tender. Add the water, chicken broth, chickpeas, diced tomatoes with their juices, cumin, cinnamon and black pepper. Bring to a boil, cover, reduce heat and simmer for 5 minutes. Add the ditalini and cook until tender. Stir in the parsley. Serves 6.

Tanya "Toni" Little
Frisco, TX

Mushroom Soup

2 oz. dried mushrooms (about 1 cup)
2 tbsp. butter
6 to 8 oz. fresh mushrooms (trimmed and sliced)
salt / pepper
2 tbsp. chopped onion (shallots)
1 cup heavy cream
2 tsp. lemon juice, or to taste

Put dried mushrooms in a saucepan with 5 cups of water. Bring to a boil, cover, turn heat to low and simmer about 10 minutes or until tender. Meanwhile, put butter in a skillet and turn heat to medium-high. When butter melts, add fresh mushrooms. Cook, stirring occasionally and seasoning with salt and pepper until they give up liquid and begin to brown. When dried mushrooms are tender, use a slotted spoon to transfer them to the skillet. Add onion. When all fresh mushrooms are browned and onions are tender, turn off heat. Strain mushroom soaking liquid through a strainer lined with cheesecloth, napkin or towel. Measure and add water or stock to make at least 4 cups. Rinse saucepan and return liquid to it. Add mushrooms and cream, and heat through. Taste and adjust seasoning. Add lemon juice. Taste once more and serve. Yield: 4 servings

Ann DeMarco
John Paul 1 Lodge #2427

Minestre

Panara
Bread Soup

1/2 cup chopped fresh herbs:
    use a combination of rosemary,
    thyme, basil, sage, arugula,
    and parsley
2 zucchini, coarsely chopped
1/2 lb. fresh green beans,
    cut in 1 inch length
1 lb. potatoes, peeled and
    cut into chunks
2 ripe tomatoes, peeled and
    coarsely chopped
1 clove garlic, peeled and crushed
1 white onion, coarsely chopped
salt / pepper
2 (1 inch) slices country bread,
    crusts removed, cut into
    3/4 inch cubes
1/2 small dried hot chile pepper
1/2 cup extra virgin olive oil
herbs for garnish

In a stockpot, combine herbs, zucchini, green beans, potatoes, tomatoes, garlic and onion. Cover with water, add salt to taste and bring to a simmer over high heat. Reduce the heat to medium-low and cook, covered, until the potatoes are tender, about 20 to 30 minutes. Soak bread briefly in the stockpot water, then squeeze to get rid of excess liquid. Crumble soaked bread and add to soup along with chile pepper.

Cook, stirring with a wooden spoon until the bread has broken down and thickened the soup, about 10 minutes longer. Season with salt and pepper to taste. Serve immediately, topped with olive oil and fresh green herbs.

Note: 1 1/2 cups canned tomatoes can be substituted for the ripe tomatoes.

Rocky Martocci
Central Gulf Coast Lodge #2708

Passatelli
Egg and Parmesan Strands in Broth

7 cups homemade meat broth
3/4 cup freshly grated Parmigiano-Reggiano cheese
1/3 cup unseasoned bread crumbs
whole nutmeg for grating
1 lemon peel, grated
2 eggs

Bring the broth to a steady, slow boil in an uncovered pot.

In the meantime, combine the grated parmesan, bread crumbs, approximately 1/8 teaspoon nutmeg, and lemon peel on a pastry board or other work surface, making a mound with a well in the center. Break the eggs into the well, and knead all the ingredients to form a granular dough, somewhat resembling polenta (cooked cornmeal mush). If the mixture is too loose and moist, add a little more grated parmesan and bread crumbs.

Fit the disk with the large holes into your food mill. When the broth begins to boil, press the passatelli mixture through the mill directly into the boiling broth, keeping the mill as high above the steam as you can. Cook at a slow, steady boil for 1 to 2 minutes.

Turn off the heat, allow the soup to settle for 4 to 5 minutes, then ladle into individual bowls. Serve with grated parmesan on the side.

Note: For best flavor, do not substitute with a commercial meat broth.

Joneanne Venable
Beaches Lodge #2821

Minestre

Pasta e Fagioli

1/2 lb. ground sirloin
1 egg
4 tbsp. seasoned bread crumbs
1 to 2 tbsp. olive oil
chopped onion
4 cloves garlic, mashed
2 cans white kidney beans
1 can navy beans
4 stalks celery with leaves, sliced thin
1 to 2 tsp. salt
1 tsp. crushed red pepper
1 tsp. black pepper
1 tsp. oregano
1 tsp. basil
1 (16 oz.) can crushed tomatoes, undrained
fresh parsley, snipped
1/2 cup carrots, julienned
1/2 lb. ditalini
grated cheese

Combine the ground meat, egg and bread crumbs. Roll into miniature balls and set aside. Heat oil in a heavy skillet over medium heat. Brown meatballs and remove. Then brown onion and garlic. Sauté gently until golden brown. Add this mixture to the beans, together with celery, salt, red and black pepper, oregano and basil. Cover and simmer 30 to 60 minutes. Check frequently. If necessary, add more water. During the last 1/2 hour of cooking add tomatoes and parsley. Add meatballs and carrots to the simmering soup. Cook 1/2 hour, then add ditalini pasta and cook until tender. Serve with grated cheese.

Joyce Stillo
Central Gulf Coast Lodge #2708

Potato Soup

4 large potatoes
4 tbsp. butter
1 small onion
2 large stalks celery, chopped
1 clove garlic
1 carrot, diced
1 1/2 tbsp. chopped parsley
1 cup tomato sauce
4 cups water
1/2 tsp. salt
1/2 tsp. pepper
3 tbsp. grated parmesan

Boil potatoes until cooked; peel and mash. In a separate pan, melt the butter, then add onion, celery, garlic, carrot and parsley. Cook until mixture starts to brown. Take out garlic and add tomato sauce, water, salt, pepper and mashed potatoes. Let simmer for 20 minutes and serve with the grated parmesan.

Dennis Piasio
Lake Worth/Boynton Beach Lodge #2304

Minestre

Spinach and Meatball Soup

1/2 lb. ground veal
1/2 lb. ground sirloin
1 egg, beaten
1/4 cup bread crumbs
1 tbsp. chopped fresh parsley
salt / pepper
4 cups chicken stock
2 cups spinach leaves, torn
1/4 cup pecorino romano cheese

Preheat oven to 350 degrees. Combine ground meats, egg, bread crumbs, parsley, salt and pepper; mix and form marble size meat balls. Bake in oven 30 minutes. Drain off fat. In a large pot bring broth to a boil. Add spinach; cover and boil for 5 minutes. Add meat balls to the hot broth; simmer for 5 minutes. Stir in the romano cheese and serve.

Sam Pittaro
Delray Beach Lodge #2719

Tortellini Soup

butter, margarine, or oil
1 small onion
chopped garlic
2 large cans chicken broth
1 (28 oz.) can tomatoes, chopped
2 cups water
Italian sausage, cooked (optional)
1 (16 oz.) pkg. cheese tortellini
carrots (optional)
1 (10 oz.) pkg. chopped spinach
1 tsp. dried basil
salt / pepper
grated parmesan

In a soup pot, sauté onion in butter until translucent. Add garlic and cook together for about 1 minute. Add chicken broth, tomatoes and water. Bring to a boil. If using sausage, add now. Add frozen tortellini, carrots and spinach. Cook until tender. Add basil, salt and pepper. Serve with grated cheese.
Note: Substitute 1 large can of V8 juice for canned tomatoes and water.

Annnette Fuoco
Delray Beach Lodge #2719

Minestre

Zuppa di Escarole
Escarole Soup

1/3 cup olive oil
2 or 3 cloves garlic, chopped
1 medium onion, diced
1 large head escarole
1 quart chicken broth (optional)

1/2 cup small shells (optional)
1 can cannellini beans
salt / pepper
grated cheese

In a large 6 quart pot simmer garlic and onion in olive oil. Wash and drain escarole, and cut into 2 inch pieces or strips. Mix escarole with onions and garlic. Simmer 5 minutes. Add 1 quart water or chicken broth. Bring to a boil for 15 minutes. Add pasta and beans, and cook until tender. Season with salt and pepper. Serve with grated cheese.

Margaret Scarfia
John Paul I Lodge #2427

Minestre

Personal Recipes:

Minestre

Personal Recipes:

Pane e Pizza

Charles J Bonaparte Lodge 2504
Cape Coral

Port Charlotte Lodge 2507
Port Charlotte

Osceola County Lodge 2523
Kissimmee

Greater Daytona Beach Lodge 2524
Port Orange

Sgt. F. M. Bonnano Lodge 2549
Boca Raton

Cinnamon Bread Ring
for Bread Machine

Bread:
1 cup warm milk
1/2 cup warm water
2 eggs, beaten
1/2 cup margarine, melted
3 tbsp. sugar
1 tsp. salt
2 tsp. orange rind
2 tsp. lemon rind
5 1/2 cups flour
2 pkgs. dry yeast

Filling:
6 tbsp. butter or margarine, softened
2/3 cup sugar
cinnamon

Put all bread ingredients in a bread machine pan in the order stated. Set machine on 'dough'. When completed, punch dough down and turn out onto a lightly floured surface. Cover and let rest for 10 minutes (or cover and refrigerate up to 24 hours, remove from refrigerator, let dough stand covered at room temperature for 15 minutes). In a small mixing bowl stir together softened butter or margarine, sugar and cinnamon. Set aside. Lightly grease a 10 inch fluted or tube pan. Set aside.

On a lightly floured surface roll dough into a 20 x 12 inch rectangle. Spread filling evenly over dough to within 1/2 inch of edge. Roll up, jelly roll style, starting from long side. Seal seam. Carefully place roll, seam side down, in prepared pan, bringing ends together to form a ring. Cover and let rise in a warm place until nearly double in size (about 45 minutes).

Bake in a 350 degree oven for 50 to 55 minutes or until golden, covering with foil the last 15 minutes of baking to prevent overbrowning. Carefully invert baking pan onto a wire rack. Remove bread from pan and cool thoroughly.

Optional: Drizzle with powdered sugar icing: In a small bowl combine 1 cup sifted powdered sugar, 1 tablespoon milk and 1/4 teaspoon vanilla. Stir in additional milk, 1 teaspoon at a time, until icing reaches a drizzling consistency.

Ann DeMarco
John Paul 1 Lodge #2427

Pane e Pizze

Easy Sausage Bread

2 bags pizza dough
1 lb. bulk sausage
1/2 cup provolone cheese
1/2 cup mozzarella cheese

1 egg
1/2 tsp. parsley
1/2 tsp. oregano
1/4 tsp. garlic salt

Take dough from refrigerator 1 hour before preparation time. Fry sausage (or remove casing before frying). Let the cooked sausage cool in a bowl until the grease settles to the bottom, to keep the bread from becoming too greasy.

Filling: Chop cheeses finely and mix with cooked sausage. Add egg and seasonings, mixing well. Spread dough on ungreased cookie sheet. Spread mixture evenly over dough and roll up into long loaves of bread. Bake at 350 degrees for 20 to 30 minutes or until golden brown. Yield: 2 loaves

Betty Chiacofuco
Rome, NY

Sausage Bread

1 pizza dough
1 lb. Italian pork sausage
8 oz. mozzarella,
    grated or cubed
1/4 cup parmesan cheese

2 eggs
1 tsp. parsley
1 tsp. oregano
salt / pepper

Skin sausage and cook over low heat until cooked. Remove from heat and drain. In a large bowl combine sausage, mozzarella, parmesan, one whole egg and egg white from second egg. Mix well. Add parsley, oregano, and salt and pepper to taste. Roll dough into a pizza circle. Spread sausage mixture on half of dough to within 1 inch of edge. Fold over other half of dough and press edge all around until it is sealed. Spread beaten egg yolk on top of dough. Place on cookie sheet and bake at 350 degrees for 45 minutes or until golden brown.

Francis D. Erasmo
Central Gulf Coast Lodge #2708

Italian Bread Ring

1 cup shredded mozzarella
1/3 cup olive oil
1/4 cup chopped fresh parsley
2 tbsp. minced onion
2 tbsp. grated romano cheese
   (or any Italian grating cheese)
1 small clove garlic
1/4 tsp. fresh basil,
   chopped fine or crushed
1 loaf ring style Italian bread
   (or use standard long loaf)

Combine ingredients, except bread, in a bowl and blend well. Cut bread into 1 inch slices, cutting almost through to bottom. Spread cheese filling between slices. Bake at 350 degrees for 10 minutes or until bread is heated and cheese is melted.

Pauline Nicolosi
Delray Beach Lodge #2719

Pepper Rolls

2 tbsp. (2 pkg.) active dry yeast
2 1/2 cups warm water
1 tbsp. olive oil
1 tbsp. salt
1 tbsp. coarse ground black pepper
6 1/2 to 7 cups flour
1 egg, beaten with 1 tsp. water
sesame seeds

In a large bowl dissolve the yeast in warm water and let stand 10 minutes until yeast is foamy. Add oil, salt, pepper. Add flour one cup at a time mixing with your hands until a ball is formed. Not all flour may be needed. Turn the dough onto a floured surface and knead until elastic, 10 to 15 minutes. Place the dough in an oiled bowl, cover with a cloth and let rise in a warm place for 1 hour. Preheat oven to 375 degrees. Grease 2 baking sheets. Punch dough down. Break off pieces and shape into round rolls about 2 inches in diameter, 1/2 inch thick. Place 2 inches apart on baking sheets, brush with egg wash, and sprinkle with sesame seeds. Cover loosely with cloth and let rise 20 minutes until doubled in size. Bake 15 to 20 minutes until golden brown.

Sam Pittaro
Delray Beach Lodge #2719

Pane e Pizze

Pane alle Olive ed Origano
Olive and Oregano Bread

This bread is excellent with salads and soups, particularly good served with an olive oil based dipping sauce. It is at its best the day it is made.

1 1/4 cups warm water, (110 - 115 degrees)	1 tsp. salt
1 tsp. active dry yeast	1/4 tsp. freshly ground black pepper
1 pinch of sugar	1/2 cup pitted black olives, coarsely chopped
1 tbsp. olive oil	
1 medium yellow onion, chopped	4 tsp. fresh oregano, minced
4 cups bread flour	4 tsp. fresh parsley, minced

Put half of the warm water in a measuring cup. Sprinkle the yeast on top. Add sugar, mix well and allow to stand for 10 minutes.

Heat the olive oil in a frying pan and fry the onion over medium heat until golden brown.

Sift the flour into a mixing bowl with the salt and pepper. Make a well in the center. Add the yeast mixture, the fried onion with the oil, the olives, herbs, and the remaining water. Gradually incorporate the flour and mix to a soft dough, adding a little extra water if necessary.

Turn out the dough onto a floured work surface and knead for 5 minutes until smooth and elastic. Place in a mixing bowl, cover with a damp dish towel and leave in a warm place to rise for about 2 hours until doubled in bulk. Lightly grease a baking sheet. Turn out the dough onto a floured surface and knead again for a few minutes. Shape into an 8 inch round and place on the prepared baking sheet. Using a sharp knife, make crisscross cuts over the top. Cover and leave in a warm place for 30 minutes until well risen. Preheat the oven to 425 degrees.

Bake for 10 minutes, then lower the oven temperature to 400 degrees. Bake for approximately 25 minutes more, or until the loaf sounds hollow when it is tapped underneath. Transfer to a wire rack and allow to cool slightly before cutting and serving. Serves 8 to 10.

Joneanne Venable
Beaches Lodge #2821

Pizza Fritta
Fried Dough

When my mom was making bread, she would just pinch some dough off, stretch it and make a doughnut out of it and fry. Just so happened she was normally doing this when we kids got home from school. What a treat it was to have that hot with sugar on it – not powdered sugar, just regular!

4 cups flour	1/4 cup dry milk
1 pkg. dry yeast	1 tbsp. Crisco
1 1/2 tbsp. sugar	1 1/2 cups warm water
1 tsp. salt	

In large bowl combine flour, yeast, sugar, salt and dry milk. Mix thoroughly by hand. Make a well in mixture and add Crisco and warm water to center of well. Mix until all ingredients are well mixed. Dough will appear wet and sticky. Cover with a cloth and set aside in a warm place to rise for 1 hour. Punch down twice. In a very large frying pan add enough oil to deep fry dough. Cut small portions of dough and form a doughnut. Do not fry too fast or on high heat. Turn to brown evenly on both sides. Put additional sugar in a bag and shake pizza fritta until the sugar coats the doughnuts.

Gloria Scalzitti Walker
Joseph B. Franzalia Lodge #2422

Garlic Bread

1 lb. butter	1 tbsp. basil or oregano
4 to 5 cloves garlic	1 loaf Italian bread
1 small jar capers, drained	mozzarella cheese slices

Mix in a processor the butter, garlic, capers, and basil or oregano. Process until well blended. Take a loaf of Italian bread, slice, but don't slice all the way. Spread the butter between the slices. Put a slice of cheese in between each slice. Wrap halfway with foil. Bake at 350 degrees for 20 minutes.

Mary Sorci
John Paul I Lodge #2427

Pane e Pizze

Personal Recipes:

Le Uova

Port St. Lucie Lodge 2594
Port St. Lucie

Marietta Lodge 2607
Marietta, Georgia

Township Lodge 2624
Coconut Creek

Marion County Lodge 2648
Ocala

Young Italians Lodge 2668
Tampa

Frittata di Funghi
Mushroom Omelet

1/2 lb. mushrooms, sliced
6 tbsp. olive oil
6 eggs
1/2 tsp. salt
1/4 tsp. pepper
3 tbsp. grated parmesan cheese

Sauté mushrooms in 2 tablespoons olive oil over low flame for 5 minutes, drain. Beat eggs with salt and pepper in a bowl. Put remainder of oil in the pan. Cook egg mixture over low flame 4 to 5 minutes. Cover with drained mushrooms. Fold omelet and cook a few minutes. Sprinkle with cheese and serve while hot. Serves 4.
Variation: In place of mushrooms, use spinach, onions, or potatoes.

Margaret Scarfia
John Paul I Lodge #2427

Fritatta Primavera

3 tbsp. butter
1 cup diced potatoes
1 cup chopped onion
1 cup small white mushrooms, sliced
12 oz. cooked asparagus, cut in 1/2 inch pieces (reserve tips)
1 cup diced ham (optional)
salt / pepper
2 1/2 cups shredded mozzarella
1 cup ricotta whole milk cheese
1/2 cup grated parmesan cheese
1 1/2 cups Half & Half
1/2 cup chopped parsley
12 large eggs, beaten

Preheat oven to 350 degrees. Melt butter in a nonstick skillet. Cook potato, onion, mushrooms over medium heat until tender. Add asparagus and ham, salt and pepper. Spread mixture into a sprayed 9 x 13 inch baking dish. Stir cheeses, cream, parsley, salt and pepper into beaten eggs. Pour egg mixture into baking dish and top with asparagus tips. Bake 45 to 55 minutes until set in middle. Cool 10 minutes before serving.

Mary Sorci
John Paul I Lodge #2427

Le Uova

My Sister's Omelette

I think my brother-in-law Joe learned this in the Navy and taught my sister Eleanor.

2 tbsp. butter
2 small potatoes, diced fine
4 large eggs
3 pinches of salt

1 pinch of pepper
1 tbsp. milk
1 tbsp. grated parmesan

Melt butter in a pan and brown potatoes. Stir eggs with salt, pepper, milk and cheese, and add to the potatoes. Cook over medium heat for 10 minutes on each side.

Dennis Piasio
Lake Worth/Boynton Beach Lodge #2304

Omelette

Cut up 4 zucchini in small pieces. Do the same with about 3 potatoes. Add to olive oil. When done, stir in about 4 eggs, salt, pepper, and a little milk. Pour into the pan, cook for 3 minutes, then turn over and cook the other side for 3 to 5 minutes.

Jeanette D'Amato

Sunday Morning Eggs

On days my father didn't have to work in the garden, he would sometimes surprise us with this delicious dish. We still reminisce about this treat.

8 slices toasted bread
1/2 stick salted butter

8 eggs, separate whites
1/2 tsp. salt

After toasting the bread, spread with butter. Beat the egg whites with salt until stiff. Pile whites on top of the toast. Press an indentation in the egg whites with a teaspoon and place an egg yolk in the center. Place in a hot oven for about 5 minutes or when egg whites brown lightly. The yolks remain nice and hot and soft. Eat and enjoy while still hot.

Dennis Piasio
Lake Worth/Boynton Beach Lodge #2304

Le Uova

Spaghetti Frittata

1 tsp. olive oil
4 slices prosciutto
   or diced ham
6 large eggs
3 tbsp. grated Parmigiano
   -Reggiano cheese

salt / pepper
1/4 cup freshly chopped basil
2 cups cooked spaghetti
1 1/2 cups cubed mozzarella
1/4 cup olive oil
4 tbsp. butter

Sauté meat in the olive oil until crispy, drain on brown paper. In a bowl beat the eggs, grated cheese, salt and pepper, and basil. Add spaghetti and mix well. Stir in the mozzarella and meat. In a 9-inch frying pan heat 2 tablespoons oil and 2 tablespoons butter. Add the mixture and smooth the top. Cook over medium-low heat until frittata is brown on the bottom and set in place. Cover pan with a large plate and invert. Add remaining oil and butter, and return frittata to pan to brown other side. Shake pan to prevent sticking. Remove, cut into wedges and serve at room temperature.

Sam Pittaro
Delray Beach Lodge #2719

Scrambled Eggs and Pepperoni

18 eggs (3 eggs per person),
   well beaten
1 small splash whole milk

pepperoni, enough to cover
   bottom of a 12 inch fry pan;
   cut into round slices, then cut
   into halves

Place pepperoni into fry pan - do not use oil. The pepperoni, when cooked, makes oil, it's what gives flavor to the eggs. You will pour off some of the oil, depending on which pepperoni you use. If you like your eggs really spicy, keep oil in the pan (you'll have eggs that are more orange.)

Watch the cooking time - don't let pepperoni get hard and leathery. When oil begins to come out it's almost done. This is definitely a dish cooked to taste. Add egg mixture and stir for about 5 to 10 minutes until totally smooth and soft, no clumps. This is a trial and error technique. *Variation:* You can add 2 slices American cheese, torn into pieces, to eggs for a slightly different taste. Add when eggs are over halfway cooked. Serves 6.

Bob Mauro
Beaches Lodge #2821

Le Uova

Personal Recipes:

Pasta e Riso

A. Edward Testa Lodge 2679
Boynton Beach

Societa d'Italia Lodge 2698
Sarasota

Loggia Mona Lisa Lodge 2699
Tampa

Cuore d'Italia Lodge 2703
Jupiter

Pompano Beach Lodge 2704
Deerfield Beach

Arugula Marinara Sauce

olive oil
garlic
crushed tomatoes

2 bunches arugula, washed
salt
1/2 lb. spaghetti

Make a sauce with olive oil, garlic and crushed tomatoes. Bring water for pasta to a boil. Add arugula, some salt, and spaghetti. When done, drain and add to the sauce.

Jeanette D'Alessandro
Township Lodge #2624

Bigole

1/2 lb. ground beef
1/2 lb. sweet Italian sausage
 (remove casing)
1 medium onion, grated
2 to 3 tsp. tomato paste

1 tbsp. sugar
1/2 to 3/4 cup beef broth
salt / pepper
1/4 cup pine nuts
2 tbsp. butter

Brown the beef and drain off any fat. Brown the sausage and drain. If sausage pieces are too thick, put them in a blender just for a second. The sausage should be the same size as the beef. Brown the onion in a little butter. Add the meat, tomato paste, sugar, and about 1/4 cup water. Simmer for about 20 minutes. This is a thick sauce, but can be diluted as desired with 1/2 to 3/4 cup beef broth. Add salt and pepper to taste. When the sauce is done, add the pine nuts and butter. Serve over hot pasta. Serves 4.

Marie Gennaci
Sgt. F. M. Bonnano Lodge #2549

Salsa

Ragu Bolognese alla Rocchina's Mamma

1/4 cup extra virgin olive oil
4 tbsp. butter
2 medium onions, finely chopped
4 stalks celery, finely chopped
1 carrot, peeled, finely chopped
5 cloves garlic, sliced
1 lb. ground veal
1 lb. ground pork
1/2 lb. ground beef
1/4 lb. ground pancetta
1/2 cup milk
1 (16 oz.) can whole, peeled
    tomatoes, with the juice
1 cup dry white wine
2 cups broth
salt / pepper

In a 6 to 8 quart, heavy-bottomed saucepan, heat olive oil and butter over medium heat. Add onion, celery, carrot and garlic, and sweat over medium heat until vegetables are tender. Add veal, pork, beef and pancetta. Stir nicely into the vegetables. Brown over high heat, stirring to keep the meat from sticking together; this should take 15 to 20 mintues. Add the milk and simmer until reduced to nothing, about 10 minutes. Add tomatoes, crushed by hand, and simmer 15 minutes. Add the wine and broth, bring to a boil, lower the heat and simmer for 2 to 2 1/2 hours. Season with salt and pepper to taste. Remove from heat.

Rocky Martocci
Central Gulf Coast Lodge #2708

Bolognese Sauce

2 tbsp. olive oil
1 clove garlic, chopped
1 lb. chopped meat, any kind
    (beef, pork or veal)
1/3 cup Marsala wine
1 (4 oz.) can sliced mushrooms
1 (28 oz.) can crushed tomatoes
2 tbsp. chopped parsley
salt / pepper

Sauté garlic and meat in hot olive oil until browned. Add wine and mushrooms and cook for 2 to 3 minutes. Add tomatoes, parsley, salt and pepper to taste. Simmer covered for approximately 40 minutes. Serve hot over pasta of your choice.

Mary Ann Rawdon
St. Augustine Lodge #2780

Marinara Sauce

1/2 cup chopped onion
1 garlic clove, minced
1/4 cup olive oil
3 cups canned Italian tomatoes, drained
1 tsp. oregano
4 fresh basil leaves
1/4 cup red wine
1 tsp. salt
black pepper, freshly ground

Sauté onion and garlic in olive oil for 5 minutes. Add remaining ingredients. Bring to a boil, reduce heat and simmer for 30 minutes, stirring occasionally.

Jean Fineberg
John Paul I Lodge #2427

Salsa di Noci

This recipe is from the Liguria region in Italy. They use a pasta called 'pansoti', in place of the ravioli.

2 to 3 cups fresh walnuts
2 to 3 cloves garlic
parmesan cheese, cubed
1/2 pint heavy cream
1 lb. cheese ravioli (small size)
parmesan cheese, grated

Place walnuts, garlic, and cubed cheese into a blender. Pulse to grind slightly. With the blender on low speed, slowly pour cream over the ingredients to form a sauce. Pour over the cooked ravioli, toss and serve immediately with grated cheese.

Theresa Branciforte
Mike Accardi Lodge #2441

Salsa

Summer Pasta Sauce

olive oil
garlic, finely chopped
leeks, sliced thin
porcini mushrooms, sliced
cremini mushrooms, sliced
zucchini, sliced
plum tomatoes, peeled and chopped
salt, pepper, oregano, thyme, rosemary

Put olive oil in a large skillet, add garlic, then leeks. Sauté mushrooms and zucchini. Lastly, add tomatoes and simmer uncovered. Add seasonsings to taste, cover and cook for a while longer. Serve over vermicelli or capellini.

Theresa Branciforte
Mike Accardi Lodge #2441

Vegetable Pasta Sauce

2 cups sliced zucchini
1 medium onion, sliced
2 tbsp. olive oil
1 (28 oz.) can crushed tomatoes
1 tsp. oregano
8 oz. mozzarella, shredded or cubed
1 lb. cooked ziti

Sauté zucchini and onion in olive oil until wilted. Add tomatoes and oregano. Simmer for 15 minutes. Add the mozzarella and serve over pasta.

Gelsie Jacobellis
Key West Lodge #2436

Angel Hair Pasta with Chicken

2 tbsp. olive oil, divided
2 skinless, boneless chicken breast halves, in 1 inch cubes
1 carrot, sliced diagonally into 1/4 inch pieces
1 (10 oz.) pkg. broccoli florets, thawed
2 cloves garlic, minced
12 oz. angel hair pasta
2/3 cup chicken broth
1 tsp. dried basil
1/4 cup parmesan cheese

Heat 1 tablespoon olive oil in a medium skillet over medium heat. Add chicken and cook, stirring until chicken is cooked thoroughly, about 5 minutes. Remove from skillet and drain on paper towels. Heat remaining oil in same skillet. Begin heating water for pasta. Add carrot pieces to skillet and cook for 4 minutes. Add broccoli and garlic to skillet. Cook, stirring for 2 minutes. Cook pasta according to package. To the skillet, add chicken broth and basil, simmer for 4 minutes. Drain pasta. Place in a large serving bowl; top with chicken, vegetable mixture, and parmesan. Serves 4.

Grace Brooks
Nature Coast Lodge #2502

Gnocchi

1/2 cup farina
2 cups hot milk
1/2 tsp. salt
1 tbsp. butter
1 egg, beaten
1 cup grated romano cheese, separated
2 cups seasoned tomato sauce

Stir farina into hot milk, add salt. Keep stirring with a wooden spoon until the farina begins to thicken. Cook slowly over low heat for 15 minutes. Remove from heat. Add butter, egg and 1/2 cup grated cheese. Mix well. Turn into a well-buttered square dish. Chill until firm. Cut into squares. Remove squares with a spatula and arrange them in a buttered baking dish. Heat tomato sauce and pour over farina squares. Sprinkle with remaining 1/2 cup grated cheese. Bake in a preheated 325 degree oven for 25 minutes. Serve hot.

Congetta Leccese
John Paul I Lodge #2427

Pasta

Baked Gnocchi

4 cups milk
1 1/2 cups semolina
1 cup grated parmesan cheese, separated
1/4 cup butter, separated
2 egg yolks, slightly beaten
1 tbsp. salt

Butter a 13 x 9 inch baking dish. Heat milk in a medium saucepan. When milk begins to boil, reduce heat and add semolina very slowly, whisking quickly to avoid lumps. Cook 10 to 15 minutes over medium-low heat, stirring constantly with a whisk (semolina is cooked when it sticks heavily to the whisk). Remove from heat. Add 1/3 cup parmesan cheese, 3 tablespoons butter, egg yolks, and salt. Mix quickly until well blended.

Moisten a work surface or a large dish with water. Pour semolina mixture onto the surface and spread it 1/2 inch thick with a wet spatula. Let it cool. Preheat oven to 400 degrees. With a small glass or cookie cutter, cut cooled semolina mixture into 2 inch rounds. Arrange in buttered baking dish, overlapping rounds slightly. Dot with about 1 tablespoon butter and sprinkle with remaining cheese (if preparing a few days in advance, simply refrigerate until ready to use). Bake 10 to 15 minutes until golden. For a golden crust, put briefly under a preheated broiler. Serve hot.

Ann DeMarco
John Paul I Lodge #2427

Pasta and Arugula

2 cloves garlic
3 tbsp. olive oil
1 can crushed tomatoes
seasoning
3 bunches arugula, washed
1/2 lb. spaghetti or ziti pasta

Sauté the garlic in olive oil. Add the tomatoes and seasoning, and cook about 40 minutes. Cook the arugula for 5 minutes, then add to the pasta. Cook together, then drain and add the tomato sauce.

Jeanette D'Alessandro
Township Lodge #2624

Capellini with Sausage and Spinach

2 tsp. olive oil
1 lb. sweet sausage,
   cut into thick slices
1 large onion, finely chopped
2 large garlic cloves, minced
2 (14 oz.) cans chicken broth
1/4 cup water

8 oz. capellini or vermicelli pasta,
   broken in half
2 (10 oz.) bags fresh spinach,
   coarsely chopped
1/2 tsp. black or red pepper
1/2 cup whipping cream

Heat oil in a dutch oven over medium heat. Add sausage and cook 3 to 4 minutes or until lightly browned. Add the onion and garlic. Cook for a few minutes. Add broth and water to the pot; cover and bring to a boil. Add pasta and cook about 3 minutes, stirring frequently. Add the spinach into the pasta and sauce, and cook for 3 minutes more, until pasta is al dente and spinach is wilted. Stir in the pepper and cream, and serve immediately.

Terry Albanese

Pasta Napoli

2 tbsp. olive oil
3 large onions, diced
2 cloves garlic, minced
1 lb. green beans, trimmed and
   cut into 1/2 inch lengths
1/2 cup vegetable broth
1/4 cup red wine

1 tbsp. fresh Italian herbs
1 tsp. salt
1/2 tsp. freshly ground pepper
1 cup chopped sun dried
   or fresh tomatoes
1 lb. rotini, cooked al dente
1/2 cup ricotta cheese

Heat oil in a large skillet over medium heat. Sauté onion and garlic until golden and fragrant, about 3 minutes. Add green beans, broth, wine, herbs, salt and pepper. Cook until beans are cooked through, stirring occasionally, about 5 minutes. Stir in tomatoes; cook until heated through, about 1 minute. Put pasta in a large serving bowl and add bean-tomato mixture. Before serving, place cheese on top. Serves 6.

Irene Lamano
St. Cloud/Kissimmee Lodge #2731

Pasta

Due Fettuccine con Prosciutto

8 oz. fettuccine
8 oz. tomato basil fettuccine
4 oz. butter
1 cup olive oil
2 (16 oz.) cans artichoke hearts, drained and chopped
3 garlic cloves, minced
1 (16 oz.) can sliced black olives, drained
1/2 lb. prosciutto, sliced
salt / pepper
parmesan cheese, grated

Cook all the fettuccine in boiling water until al dente. Melt the butter in a sauté pan or 10 inch skillet. Add the olive oil, artichoke hearts, garlic, olives and prosciutto. Sauté until heated through. Drain fettuccine and place in a serving bowl. Add the prosciutto mix and toss well. Season with salt and pepper to taste. Serve immediately with grated cheese. Serves 8.

Ann DeMarco
John Paul I Lodge #2427

Rigatoni with Onion Sauce

1 lb. rigatoni
1/4 lb. thick bacon, finely diced
1 large white onion, thinly sliced
1 tbsp. flour
1 1/2 cups beef broth
6 tbsp. Parmigiano-Reggiano
2 tsp. coarsely ground black pepper

Cook the rigatoni for 10 to 12 minutes until firm. Drain and keep warm. In a large skillet, sauté bacon and onion until browned. Sprinkle the flour over and mix to blend. Stir in the rigatoni. Add half the beef stock and stir 10 minutes. Add cheese and remaining stock. Remove from heat. Stir in black pepper. Serve at once.
\

Sam Pittaro
Delray Beach Lodge #2719

Pasta and Ceci

This tasty old Italian 'peasant' dish is an old standard that was used to fill hungry bellies without having to spend a lot of money on ingredients. Today, the dish is considered a 'healthy' dish, and still a welcome one to people who remember the old times, and like the taste of ceci beans.

1 (12 or 16 oz.) pkg. dry ceci (garbanzo) beans
1/3 cup olive oil
1 large onion, peeled and chopped
3 garlic cloves, peeled and whole
1 1/2 cups chopped celery
a few sprigs Italian parsley, chopped
1 lb. pasta – Mafalde (or other type pasta)
grated parmesan cheese
red pepper flakes

Sort the ceci beans the day before you want to cook them; put the beans in a pot or plastic container, cover with water and soak overnight to help them soften. Drain the soaked beans, put in a pot, and cover with water. Cook, adding more water if beans become dry. Cook until beans are tender and cooked. Set beans aside but do not drain out cooking liquids. While beans are cooking, in another pan, sauté onion, garlic, and celery in olive oil until vegetables are lightly browned. Add this vegetable mixture to the cooked ceci beans and mix together. Add chopped parsley. Cook pasta in boiling salted water until just tender. Drain water from pasta, and add the pasta to the ceci bean mixture. Stir and let sit 5 minutes to let liquids soak into pasta. Serve hot with grated cheese and red pepper flakes, if desired. Serves 8 to 10.

Nancy DeGregory
Sgt. F. M. Bonnano Lodge #2549

Mom's Favorite Spaghetti Pie

1 lb. spaghetti
6 eggs
3/4 cup Italian cheese, grated
1/3 cup oil for frying

Cook spaghetti and drain with cold water. Place in a bowl, add eggs and cheese. Mix well. In a large frying pan, heat oil until hot. Then add spaghetti mixture carefully, cooking until bottom is crisp. Place a dish on top of the mixture and turn over to brown the other side. Serve hot.

Anne Cristodero
John Paul I Lodge #2427

Pasta

Polenta Filled Manicotti

marinara sauce　　　　　　　　shredded mozzarella cheese
grated parmesan cheese

Crepes:

- 6 eggs
- 2 cups milk
- 1 tsp. salt
- 1 cup flour
- 6 tbsp. butter, divided

Whisk eggs, milk, and salt in a medium bowl to blend. Add flour and whisk until smooth. Whisk in 2 tablespoons butter. Heat a 5 inch diameter skillet over medium heat. Brush with some melted butter. Pour 2 tablespoons batter into the skillet and swirl to coat the bottom. Cook until the edge of the crepe is light brown, about 30 seconds. Loosen edges gently, and carefully turn the crepe over. Cook until the crepe is just cooked through, about 15 seconds. Transfer to a plate and cover with a paper towel. Repeat with remaining batter, brushing the skillet with more melted butter. Crepes can be made ahead of the day of use and kept refrigerated.

Filling:

- 1 lb. ricotta cheese
- 3 eggs
- 1/4 cup olive oil
- 1 cup shredded parmesan cheese
- salt / pepper

Beat ingredients with mixer until creamy.

Polenta:

- 8 1/4 cups water
- 1 dash of salt
- 2 1/4 cups cornmeal

Combine water and salt in a large pot; bring to a boil. Gradually add cornmeal, whisking constantly. Reduce heat, simmer until polenta is soft and thick, whisking often, for about 8 minutes. Take off the heat for 5 minutes. Combine with the ricotta cheese filling.

Fill crepes with polenta/ricotta cheese mixture. Place your favorite marinara sauce on the bottom of a 14 x 17 inch aluminum pan. Cover the manicotti with

Pasta

sauce and bake in a 370 degree oven for 30 minutes, covered with aluminum foil. Remove the foil cover and sprinkle the top with grated parmesan and shredded mozzarella. Bake uncovered for another 30 minutes. Yield: 2 dozen

John Apice

Cannelloni

2 tbsp. olive oil
4 cloves garlic, minced
1/4 cup onion, minced
1/4 cup celery, minced
1 lb. ground veal

1 cup diced mushrooms
2 tbsp. grated parmesan cheese
2 tbsp. tomato paste
2 tbsp. chopped basil
2 tbsp. minced parsley

In a large skillet combine oil, garlic, and onion. Sauté for 2 to 3 minutes. Add celery and cook 1 minute more. Add the veal and cook until no more pink color is showing. Add the mushrooms and cook for 2 minutes. Add the parmesan cheese, tomato paste, basil and parsley. Heat through. Adjust the seasonings to taste.

Quick Tomato Sauce:

3 tbsp. olive oil
3 cloves garlic, minced
1 1/2 cups crushed tomatoes

2 tbsp. chopped basil
1 cup grated parmesan cheese
salt / pepper

6 fresh or frozen pasta sheets, thawed

Heat the oil in a saucepan; add garlic and cook 1 to 2 minutes. Add the tomatoes. If mixture is too thick, add a little water. Cook for 15 minutes. Add basil, cheese, and salt and pepper to taste.

Cut the pasta sheets into 3 x 5 inch pieces and cook in boiling water for 2 minutes. Remove from boiling water and shock in cold water. Continue until all of the sheets are done. Lay out the sheets on a flat surface and place 2 to 3 tablespoons of the meat mixture on each sheet. Roll up each sheet and place the rolls, cut side down, in a lightly oiled baking dish. Cook in a 400 degree oven for 15 minutes, serve at once. Serves 4.

Ann DeMarco
John Paul I Lodge #2427

Pasta

Orzo with Vegetables

1 tbsp. olive oil
1 tbsp. butter
9 oz. orzo pasta
1 cup finely chopped onion
3/4 cup carrots, 1/4 inch dice
2/3 cup celery, 1/4 inch dice
2 medium garlic cloves, minced

1/4 tsp. salt
1/8 tsp. black pepper
1 (14 oz.) can chicken broth
3/4 cup water
1 1/4 cups yellow squash, 1/4 inch dice
1/4 cup chopped fresh parsley

Heat the oil and butter in a deep 12 inch heavy skillet over moderately high heat until foam subsides, then sauté the orzo, stirring constantly until golden brown, 1 to 2 minutes. Add the onion, carrots, celery, garlic, salt and pepper and sauté, stirring constantly until onion is lightly browned, about 5 minutes.

Add the broth and water and bring to a boil. Reduce heat to a low setting and cook, uncovered, until the liquid is absorbed, about 20 minutes. Stir in the squash and parsley, and allow to stand 5 minutes before serving. Serves 6 as side dish.

Joneanne Venable
Beaches Lodge #2821

Golden Onion Orzo

2 tbsp. butter or margarine
1 large onion, halved, cut crosswise in 1/4 inch slices
8 oz. orzo pasta
2 cloves garlic, minced

1/4 tsp. black pepper
1/3 cup white wine
1 (14.5 oz.) can chicken broth
1/4 cup chopped parsley
3 tbsp. grated parmesan cheese

In a large pot, melt butter or margarine over medium heat. Add onion. Cook, stirring frequently until golden, 8 to 10 minutes. Stir in the orzo, garlic and pepper. Cook, stirring frequently, until orzo is lightly toasted, 1 to 2 minutes. Stir in the wine and cook until absorbed, 1 to 2 minutes. Add the broth with 1 cup water. Bring to a boil. Reduce heat to medium-low and simmer, stirring frequently until orzo is tender and most of the liquid is absorbed. Add more water if all liquid is absorbed before orzo is cooked through, 7 to 10 minutes. Stir parsley and cheese into the mixture during the last 2 minutes of cooking time. Transfer to a serving bowl.

Ann DeMarco
John Paul I Lodge #2427

Pasta

Ravioli with Stuffing

My grandfather used an old sheet laid out on the table and placed the ravioli on top of the sheet that was spread with cornmeal. He covered the ravioli with another sheet and let stand overnight to dry.

Stuffing:

- 1 1/2 lbs. or 2 pkgs. frozen chopped spinach
- 2 slices bread
- 2 tbsp. olive oil
- 1 1/2 cups parmesan cheese
- 3 eggs
- 2 cloves garlic, chopped

Cook spinach and let cook, drain all the water. Wet the bread and drain water out; add olive oil to moisten. Mix all remaining ingredients together and use to stuff ravioli. This stuffing could be used for all other kinds of stuffed pasta.

Ravioli dough:

- 1 1/2 cups flour
- 2 eggs
- 3 to 6 tbsp. water

Place flour on pastry board and make a deep well in center. Add slightly beaten eggs into well and add water and start to mix flour with eggs and additional water if necessary. Knead it out till it's smooth. Let dough stand for about 1/2 hour then roll it out on a floured work surface about 1/16 inch think. For bottom, spread filling about 1/4 inch thick and be sure filling extends to edge of dough. For the top layer, roll out another portion of dough the same size and thickness as bottom layer. Place on top of the filled layer and stretch to cover bottom layer completely. Run a rolling pin lightly over the top layer of dough to even the filling out. With either a ravioli press or a ravioli rolling pin press down firmly to seal dough layers and enclose filling in ravioli squares. With a fluted pasty wheel cut filled squares apart along imprinted lines. With a spatula transfer ravioli onto a baking pan covered lightly with cornmeal; cover and let dry overnight.

Add ravioli to salted lightly boiling water for 10 to 12 minutes and serve. Recipe can also be fozen.

Rosemary Coronato
Sgt. F. M. Bonnano Lodge #2549

Pasta

Ravioli Napoletan

My mother made these at least two times a month. They are the most tender ravioli you will ever eat.

3 cups water
2 tbsp. butter
1/2 tsp. salt

1 cup farina
5 cups flour

In a large pan, boil the water with the butter and salt. Turn heat to medium. Add farina slowly and continue stirring until the mixture leaves the sides of the pan. Cool enough to handle. Put 4 cups of flour on a board and make a well. Add farina and mix well. Knead about 5 minutes using the last cup of flour. Place in a bowl, cover and let rest 1 hour. Roll very thin, fill with a ricotta, meat, spinach or mixture of shrimp filling. Seal the edges with a fork.

Mary Sorci
John Paul I Lodge #2427

Rigatoni with Cinnamon Beef

2 lb. beef (chuck roast)
1 large grated onion
2 small cans tomato paste
1/4 cup white wine
4 tsp. sugar

1/8 tsp. ground cloves
1 tsp. ground cinnamon
1/4 tsp. pepper
3 tbsp. pecorino cheese
1 lb. rigatoni

Brown the meat in oil. Remove the meat, and in the same oil, brown the onion until golden. Put meat back in the pot and add tomato paste and wine; stir well. Add water until meat is covered. Bring to a boil, then add 2 teaspoons sugar, cloves, 1/2 teaspoon cinnamon, and pepper. Simmer until the meat is tender, about 2 hours. Remove meat from the pot. When meat is completely cooled, chop with a cleaver until meat is about the size of a grain of rice. Add to the meat the remaining 2 teaspoons sugar and 1/2 teaspoon cinnamon. Then add the pecorino cheese. Serve rigatoni with the sauce the meat was cooked in and sprinkle chopped meat on top. Serves 4.

Marie Gennaci
Sgt. F. M. Bonnano Lodge #2549

Sausage Bow Tie Pasta

6 links Italian sausage
1 green pepper
1 red pepper
1 large onion, sliced
1 (14 oz.) can chicken broth
6 large white mushrooms, cleaned and sliced
1 can black olives
1 jar marinated artichoke hearts
1/2 tsp. dried basil
1/2 tsp. Italian seasoning
1/4 tsp. garlic powder
salt / pepper
1 lb. bow tie pasta, cooked al dente

Cut the sausage and red and green peppers into bite size pieces. In a large skillet brown the sausage over medium-high heat. Set aside. In the same skillet, sauté the onions until soft. Add a little chicken broth to deglaze the skillet. Add to the sausages and reserve. In the same skillet, sauté the green and red peppers until soft, again deglazing the pan with chicken broth. Add to the reserved mixture. Repeat the process with the mushrooms. When the mushrooms are cooked, add the remaining chicken broth and the reserved sausage mixture. Bring to a low boil. Add the olives, artichoke hearts and the seasonings. Simmer for 5 minutes. Drain the pasta well and add to the skillet. Keep on low heat for 1 minute.

Tortellini with Scallops alla Michael

This recipe was given to me by my nephew, Michael, while he was an apprentice at his parents' restaurant in New Jersey.

1 lb. scallops
1/2 cup butter
1 tsp. crushed garlic
1 lb. tortellini
1/2 cup frozen peas, thawed
1/2 cup broccoli florets
2 tbsp. flour
1/2 tsp. salt
1/4 tsp. pepper
1 pint whipping cream

In a large skillet sauté scallops in butter for 10 minutes. Add garlic; sauté 5 more minutes. Cook tortellini according to directions. Cook peas and broccoli until al dente. Add flour, salt, pepper and cream to scallops until slightly thickened. Add tortellini, peas and broccoli. Stir and simmer for 30 minutes.

Marie LoSapio
Mike Accardi Lodge #2441

Pasta

Linguine with Vodka Sauce

This is a new Christmas Eve dish with shrimp for the traditional Feast of Fishes in our house.

4 tbsp. olive oil
1/2 cup minced onion
2 cloves garlic, chopped
1 (32 oz.) can crushed tomatoes
1/2 tsp. salt
1/2 tsp. pepper
1/3 cup vodka
1/2 cup heavy cream
1/4 tsp. red pepper flakes
   (optional)

In a large skillet heat oil over medium heat. Add onions and sauté until tender. Add garlic; sauté another 3 minutes. Add crushed tomatoes, salt and pepper, and cook for 15 minutes. Add vodka and continue cooking for 20 minutes longer, until vodka evaporates and sauce thickens. Add cream and cook for another 3 minutes. Serve immediately over linguine. Sprinkle with red pepper flakes.

Variations: You can add cooked shrimp to the sauce before adding cream; you can add peas and mushrooms to the sauce for a vegetarian dish.

Marie Caponero
John Paul I Lodge #2427

Pasta and Fava Beans

1 or 2 tsp. diced, crushed onion
1 garlic clove, crushed
2 tbsp. olive oil
1 (19 oz.) can Progresso fava beans
salt / pepper
1 bay leaf
1 1/2 cups ditalini or
   small shells

Sauté onions and garlic in oil. Add the can of fava beans with juice and a little water. Add salt and pepper and bay leaf. Cook about 15 minutes. Boil the pasta, then drain and add to the beans.

Jeanette D'Alessandro
Township Lodge #2624

Spaghetti with Meatballs

1 lb. spaghetti
parmesan cheese

Meatballs:

1/2 lb. chopped veal	2 tbsp. chopped fresh parsley
1/2 lb. chopped pork	2 tsp. chopped fresh basil
1/2 lb. chopped beef	1/2 tsp. salt
2 slices prosciutto, minced	1/2 tsp. pepper
1/2 cup bread crumbs	1 clove garlic, chopped fine
1/2 cup wine (any kind)	1 dash of nutmeg
1/2 cup parmesan cheese	1/4 cup olive oil
1/4 cup milk	1/4 cup flour
2 eggs, lightly beaten	

Sauce:

4 tbsp. chopped onion	1/2 tsp. salt
1 large can Italian tomatoes, peeled	dash of pepper
	3 tbsp. tomato paste
2 tsp. chopped fresh basil	

Combine the meat, prosciutto, bread crumbs, wine, cheese, milk, eggs, parsley, basil, salt, pepper, garlic and nutmeg into a food processor. Pulse a couple of times until ingredients are blended. Shape into medium size balls. Heat olive oil in a frying pan. Dredge meatballs in flour, then brown on all sides in oil. When meatballs are brown, remove from the pan and reserve oil. In the same frying pan, using the reserved oil, brown the onion until golden. Add the tomatoes, basil, salt and pepper, and simmer 30 minutes. Blend in tomato paste, return meatballs to the pan with sauce and simmer 20 minutes longer. While sauce is cooking, cook spaghetti in boiling water until tender; drain and place on a serving dish. Pour sauce over spaghetti, mix lightly, arrange meatballs on top and serve with a sprinkling of grated parmesan cheese. Serves 4 to 6.

Alfonsina Milano
John Paul I Lodge #2427

Pasta

Manicotti

Prepared tomato sauce
Italian cheese, grated

Crepes:
    5 eggs
    1 1/2 cups flour
    1 1/2 cups water
    1/2 tsp. salt

Mix ingredients together. Add more water if needed. Using a seasoned 6 inch skillet, pour enough mixture to cover the bottom of the skillet. Let it set on top. Do not turn. When cooked, place the crepe on wax paper to cool. Repeat the process until all the mixture is used.

Filling:
    1 or 2 lbs. ricotta cheese
    1 egg
    Italian cheese, grated
    1/2 tsp. chopped parsley

Mix ingredients together. Spread filling on the crepes and roll up. Spread some tomato sauce in the bottom of a baking dish. Place the manicotti on top. Cover with additional sauce, then top with Italian cheese. Bake for 30 to 35 minutes at 350 degrees.

Mary Ann Latona
John Paul I Lodge #2427

Pasta Rustica

1 1/2 lbs. Italian sausage
3 cloves garlic, chopped
olive oil
1/2 onion, chopped
3 stalks celery, chopped
4 carrots, chopped
3 portobello mushrooms, sliced

Seasonings: garlic, mixed peppers, thyme, oregano, chopped basil, red pepper
1 (16 oz.) can plum tomatoes, peeled
1/2 cup tomato paste
1 cup red wine
1 cup cream
1 lb. penne pasta

In a deep frying pan, cook the sausage meat and garlic in olive oil until brown. Add the onion, celery and carrots, and cook until glazed. Add portobello mushrooms and cook until soft. Season with additional garlic, mixed ground peppers, thyme, oregano, basil and a pinch of red pepper. Mix thoroughly. Add the plum tomatoes and tomato paste. Add 1 to 1 1/2 cups water and simmer for at least 1 hour. Taste and adjust seasoning if necessary. Add red wine. Simmer, covered, on low heat until ready for use, then add cream to the sauce and mix thoroughly.

Boil the pasta until al dente, then drain and place in a bowl. Add the sauce and mix. Serve with a topping of parmesan cheese. Makes 6 to 8 servings.

Ron and Ann Albano
Delray Beach Lodge #2719

Spinach and Pasta

This recipe is a creation of my mother, Sabastiannina Marinaccio Carozzalo, to serve eight children. It is great served with whatever side dish you want.

In a sauté pan add oil, garlic and some pepper seeds. Sauté about 5 minutes. Add 1 pound of spinach and cook until wilted. Set aside.

Make a pasta dough with just flour, water and a pinch of salt. Roll very thin. Cut in 1 inch wide strips, and then cut into 1 inch squares. Cook the pasta 5 minutes. Drain some of the water out, then add the spinach. Heat through.

Mary Sorci
John Paul I Lodge #2427

Pasta

Spaghetti and Asparagus

I grew up in rural New Jersey. The Anderson farm was next to ours and was one of the few non-Italian-owned farms in the area. I remember seeing the beautiful, fluffy ferns of the asparagus plants growing in a patch nearby. I could walk close to the plants, but never would I touch them. Year after year I would see the plants, but never do I recall our family having these asparagus to eat. Now, fresh asparagus is abundant in food markets, and we can enjoy it frozen, canned, or fresh. This is one of my favorite dishes. It is easy, quick, and fun to make. It is also light and nutritious and not that expensive.

1 lb fresh asparagus, cut diagonally, 2 inch pieces	6 oz. spaghetti (or other favorite pasta)
5 tbsp. olive oil	salt
1 small onion	grated parmesan cheese
2 garlic cloves	red pepper flakes

Discard the tough bottom pieces of asparagus. Peel and chop the onion and garlic. Heat olive oil in a frying pan. Add onion and garlic and cook until almost soft. Add asparagus; cook until asparagus is tender but still crisp. Keep the pan on low heat. In another pot, boil 2 quarts water, adding salt to taste. Cook the spaghetti until al dente.

Reserve one cup of pasta water, and then drain the spaghetti. Add the spaghetti to the asparagus mixture. Add about 1/2 cup of the pasta water and mix everything together. Cover the pan and cook another three minutes. Add more liquid if mixture becomes too dry. Turn off heat and let sit for a few minutes. Serve with grated parmesan cheese and red pepper flakes, if desired. Serves 3.

Nancy DeGregory
Sgt. F. M. Bonnano Lodge #2549

Pasta

Spaghetti con Fegatini di Pollo
Spaghetti and Chicken Livers

1 lb. fresh chicken livers
1 lb. spaghetti, cooked and drained
salt / pepper
2 cups tomato sauce
1/4 cup grated parmesan cheese

Place chicken livers in a greased baking dish. Bake in a 375 degree oven for 15 minutes until done, but not dry. Chop livers into coarse pieces. Toss with hot spaghetti. Season with salt and pepper to taste. Serve with hot tomato sauce and grated parmesan cheese. *Note:* Instead of baking the chicken livers, they can be sautéd quickly in hot butter or olive oil.

Congetta Leccese
John Paul I Lodge #2427

Stephanie's Broccoli Rabe and Sausage over Pasta

1 lb. sausage, remove casing
1 1/2 lbs. broccoli rabe
3 to 4 cloves garlic, minced
3 tbsp. olive oil
1 cup chicken broth
1 tsp. hot pepper flakes
salt / pepper
1 lb. orechiette pasta ("little ears")
romano cheese, grated

In a skillet, crumble sausage and brown over moderate to high heat. Drain grease and blot on paper towels. Set aside. Trim and discard course leaves and tough stem roots from broccoli rabe. Cut off florets. Peel large stems and cut into 1/2 inch pieces. Rinse and drain. In a large skillet, set over moderate heat, cook the garlic in the oil until lightly golden. Add the broccoli rabe, broth, hot pepper flakes, salt and pepper. Cook the mixture over moderate high heat, partially covered, stirring occasionally until broccoli is just tender and the sausage is heated through. In a pot of salted boiling water, cook the pasta until al dente. Drain. Add the broccoli rabe mixture and toss to combine. Serve with grated cheese and extra hot pepper flakes on the side. *Note:* For a healthier recipe, substitute low-fat sausage and low sodium chicken broth.
Variations: Replace sausage with 1 lb. peeled, chopped, and seeded tomatoes. To make the meal a little heartier, add 1/2 cup evaporated milk.

Delia Jones
Hollywood Commonwealth Lodge #2761

Riso

Italian Rice Balls

Quantity: 95 This recipe feeds an army!

1/2 lb. butter
1 (2 lb. 10 oz.) box white rice
chicken stock (several quarts)
salt
3 onions, chopped
1/4 cup olive oil
2 lb. chopped meat

1/2 cup chopped parsley
2 large mozzarella cheeses, diced
8 eggs
1/2 cup grated cheese
bread crumbs
oil for frying, peanut or corn

Melt butter in a large pot. Add rice, mix well, and little by little add the chicken stock. Stir constantly, adding broth until rice is cooked well. Salt to taste. Set rice aside to cool.

Sauté onions in the olive oil, then add chopped meat and parsley, cooking until meat is browned. Dice the mozzarella. Set cheese and meat mixture on your work area. Scramble 3 eggs with grated cheese and pour onto cooked rice. Mix well, and you are ready to start a day's work! Put the remaining eggs in a bowl and mix well.

Put a spoonful of rice in your hands, add some meat and a piece of mozzarella. Form a ball 2 inches or less in diameter. Roll in beaten egg, then in bread crumbs. Place on foil. When all 95 meatballs are finished, fry what you need in deep oil and freeze the rest.

Fried balls also may be frozen, reheated in an oven and kept warm on an electric hot tray for eating later.

Doris Danza

Riso

Rice Balls I

6 cups cooked rice, cold
grated cheese
black pepper
parsley

small amount of garlic
1 egg, beaten
bread crumbs
oil for frying

Combine the first 5 ingredients. The mixture should not be too wet. Form into balls, dip into the beaten egg, then roll in the bread crumbs. Fry the balls in oil heated in a deep pot.

Anne Cristodero
John Paul I Lodge #2427

Rice Balls II

1/2 lb. uncooked rice
3 tbsp. olive oil
1 lb. ground beef
salt / pepper

1/4 cup grated parmesan cheese
2 eggs, well beaten
1 cup bread crumbs
2 cups vegetable oil

Cook rice in 2 quarts boiling water until kernels crush easily between thumb and finger. Drain and cool slightly. While rice is cooking brown the meat in oil over medium heat. Season with salt and pepper. Add grated cheese and blend well; cool. Place 2 tablespoons cooked rice in the palm of your hand. Make a well in the rice and put in 1 heaping tablespoon of the meat mixture. Mold rice around the meat, making a ball. Dip balls in beaten eggs and roll in bread crumbs. Fry in deep, hot oil until golden brown, about 3 minutes. Do not fry more than 3 at a time. Remove balls from oil with a slotted spoon and serve immediately.

Ann DeMarco
John Paul I Lodge #2427

Riso

Rice Balls III

1 cup Arborio rice
3 eggs
1/4 cup grated romano cheese
3 tbsp. fresh minced parsley
1/4 cup tomato sauce
salt / pepper

1/4 cup mozzarella cheese, diced
1/2 cup browned ground beef
1/4 cup green peas
2 cups bread crumbs
peanut oil for frying

In a saucepan, bring 2 1/2 cups of water to a boil. Cook the rice for 15 minutes until firm. Drain, place in a bowl. Beat 1 egg, add to the rice with the grated cheese, parsley and 2 tablespoons tomato sauce, salt and pepper to taste. Mix well. Put in refrigerator for 15 minutes. In another bowl mix the mozzarella cheese, beef, remaining sauce and peas. With floured hands shape 10 balls. Poke a hole in the center with your finger. Fill with 1 1/2 tablespoons mozzarella mixture. Reshape and cover the hole. Beat remaining 2 eggs. Spread bread crumbs onto a plate. Dip the balls in the egg, coating all over. Roll in the bread crumbs, coating evenly. Let dry on a plate for 45 minutes. Fry in 375 degree oil until golden brown all over. Drain and serve with lemon wedges or tomato sauce.

Sam Pittaro
Delray Beach Lodge #2719

Risotto con Funghi alla Contadina
Rice and Mushrooms Country Style

2 to 3 slices bacon, finely chopped
1 onion, golf ball size
1 small bell pepper, finely chopped
1/2 tsp. oregano
black pepper, approx. 1/2 tsp.

1/2 lb. mushrooms, quartered
3 cups cooked rice
1/2 cup chicken broth
salt

Render the bacon in a large skillet. Add onion and bell pepper. Simmer for 5 minutes. Add oregano and black pepper. Simmer 15 minutes. Stir in mushrooms. Simmer 5 minutes. Before adding rice, mix well. Add broth, and salt to taste. Simmer uncovered until most of the broth has evaporated. Serves 6.

Margaret Scarfia
John Paul I Lodge #2427

Risotto

1/4 cup butter
1 medium onion, minced
2 cups rice, uncooked
6 cups chicken broth

1/8 tsp. saffron (optional)
1/2 cup parmesan cheese
salt / pepper

Melt butter in a large skillet. Add onion and sauté slowly, stirring frequently; do not allow to brown. Add rice, stirring for a minute or two. Add chicken broth, a little at a time. Add saffron. Cook for about 25 minutes, stirring occasionally until rice is tender. You may add a little water if rice sticks before done. Add cheese, and salt and pepper to taste, before serving. Serves 6 to 8.

Note: You can add vegetables, shrimp, lobster, chicken or beef. Just sauté vegetables or fish or meats in about 3 tablespoons of butter before adding to the cooked rice.

Ann DeMarco
John Paul I Lodge #2427

Risi e Bisi

This is often served in Italy in a soupy fashion. Add crisply fried chicken livers at the last minute for a more substantial meal.

1 medium onion, finely chopped
1 slice bacon, chopped
1/2 cup butter
2 tbsp. olive oil
1 1/2 cups fresh or frozen peas

3 to 4 cups hot broth
1 1/2 cups rice
salt / pepper
2 to 3 tbsp. parmesan cheese
fresh chopped parsley

Sauté the onion and bacon in butter and oil until soft or lightly golden. Add the peas and a cup of the broth, then the rice and more broth. Season with salt and pepper. Serve, sprinkled with cheese and parsley and dotted with butter.

Mary A. Sorci
John Paul I Lodge #2427

Polenta

Soft Polenta

2 quarts water
1 tbsp. salt
2 cups yellow corn meal
1/2 to 1 lb. Italian sausage
   (hot or sweet)

1 cup tomato paste,
   diluted with broth or water
6 tbsp. butter
salt / pepper
1/2 cup grated cheese

Place water and salt in a large saucepan and bring to boil. Gradually pour cornmeal, stirring constantly with a wooden spoon. Cook over medium heat approximately 20 minutes or until the consistency of mashed potatoes.

Remove casing from sausage. Sauté sausage in a little oil for 10 minutes. Add tomato mixture, butter, and salt and pepper to taste. Simmer until the sauce has reached the right consistency. Season with salt and pepper to taste.

Place polenta on a large platter. Using a tablespoon, make large indentations with the back of the spoon. Pour sauce and cheese over all and enjoy.

Margaret Scarfia
John Paul I Lodge #2427

Grandma Marietta's Ravioli

Grandma Cositore said you had to use a pin to place a small hole in each ravioli to let the air escape while cooking. Although I don't think it is absolutely necessary, that's how she made hers. My son-in-law Fred recently bought me a metal crimper, saying we needed to modernize a bit. When we made our ravioli and he tried it for the first time, he decided the old fashioned jelly glass method worked best after all! Now my husband, our children and grandchildren always get together before Christmas to make great grandma's recipe. I think the grandchildren "wear" more of the flour than we use to make the ravioli!

For approximately 120 raviolis:
9 cups flour
1 tsp. salt, more added as needed
6 eggs
6 tbsp. soft butter
2 cups water

Mix flour and salt. Place on a flat surface and make a well in the center. Add slightly beaten eggs, butter and water. Mix well and knead dough.

Filling:
4 eggs, beaten
4 lbs. ricotta
1/4 tsp. cinnamon
2/3 cup grated Italian cheese
2 1/2 tbs. minced parsley
sugar, to taste
salt and pepper, to taste

Mix all filling ingredients well and set aside. Roll out dough. Drop filling on dough by tablespoonfuls and cover with another sheet of dough. Use a small jelly glass to score and cut each ravioli. Crimp the edges of each ravioli with a fork.

To cook, add raviolis to lightly salted boiling water and cook about 10 minutes or to desired doneness.

Marie Bosco
Sister of Grand Lodge of Florida
President Dan Cositore
Societa D'Italia #2698

Salsa-Pasta-Riso-Polenta

Personal Recipes:

Carne, Pesce, Pollo

Central Gulf Coast Lodge 2708
Tarpon Springs

Italian Fellowship Lodge 2713
Royal Palm Beach

Delray Beach Lodge 2719
Delray Beach

Friendship Lodge 2728
Hudson

St. Cloud/Kissimmee Lodge 2731
St. Cloud

Carne

Bistecca alla Pizzaiola

This recipe was passed down from my grandmother in Naples, Italy. It won a prize of 4th place recently at a Tampa, FL restaurant.

1 (15 oz.) can plum
  tomatoes, chopped
2 lbs. chuck steak,
  sliced 1/2 inch thick
2 garlic cloves, chopped
salt / pepper
1 tsp. oregano
2 potatoes, cut into wedges
1 small onion, sliced
1 green pepper, sliced
1/4 cup olive oil
2 carrots, sliced (optional)
fresh basil

Preheat oven to 375 degrees. Place some canned tomatoes into a roasting pan. Place sliced steak over tomatoes. Put garlic, salt, pepper, oregano, potatoes, onion and bell pepper over meat. Cover with remaining tomatoes and olive oil.

Cover with aluminum foil and bake for 2 hours. After 1 hour, baste meat. Test meat for doneness. Carrots may be added as an additional vegetable if desired. Serves 4 to 6. *Variation:* Use a red bell pepper instead of green.

Margaret Scarfia
John Paul I Lodge #2427

Carne

Bistecca ai Peperoni
Beef Steak and Bell Peppers

1/4 cup olive oil
1 clove garlic, sliced
1 large onion, sliced
1 tsp. oregano
salt / pepper

1 to 2 lbs. top sirloin, cut in serving pieces
2 large bell peppers, cut in strips
1 cup tomatoes

In a large skillet heat the oil; add the garlic, onion, oregano (thyme is optional), and salt and pepper to taste. Simmer for 3 to 4 minutes, then add the beef. Spread the oil mixture, bell peppers and tomatoes over the meat. Lower the heat and cook until meat is tender. Add water if needed. Serves 4 to 6. *Note:* Chuck steak can be substituted for top sirloin.

Margaret Scarfia
John Paul I Lodge #2427

Garmugia

My mom still makes this delicious dish; even my granddaughter loves it.

2 tbsp. olive oil
4 small onions, chopped
1 garlic clove, chopped
2 tbsp. parsley chopped
2 lbs. diced beef
3 artichokes

2 cups fresh peas
1/2 tsp. salt
1/2 tsp. pepper
1 pinch of sugar
1/2 cup water

Sauté onions, garlic and parsley in olive oil until brown. Add the beef and cook until it is nice and brown. Remove the outer leaves of the artichokes and cut into 8 sections each. Mix with the peas and add to the pan. Add salt, pepper, sugar and water to the pan and cover. Cook over low heat for 30 minutes (or when meat is done).

Em Jay Aumais
Lake Worth/Boynton Beach Lodge #2304

Braciola

1 lb. top round steak
salt pork
fresh bread crumbs
salt / pepper
2 garlic cloves, minced

1/4 cup raisins
1/2 cup finely chopped parsley
2 tbsp. olive oil
1 quart spaghetti sauce
1/3 cup grated parmesan cheese

Cut steak into 4 to 6 pieces and pound each piece until thin. Rub each piece with salt pork, then with bread crumbs and season with salt and pepper. Add garlic, raisins and parsley. Roll each piece tightly and tie with string. Heat olive oil in a medium skillet over medium-high heat. Brown each braciola roll on all sides. Place braciola rolls in simmering spaghetti sauce and cook until tender. Serve with pasta and grated parmesan.

Tony Celona
John Paul I Lodge #2427

Mama's Beef and Peppers

My mother, Sabastiannina Marinaccio Carozzolo of Acadia, Italy made this for my dad for lunch.

Boil a 2 to 3 pound chuck roast. When tender, remove from the broth and save the broth for soup.

Cut the roast into chunks and put some olive oil into a sauté pan. Add the beef pieces and 1 jar of sliced hot and sweet pickled peppers. Sauté about 15 minutes. Serve with crusty Italian bread and a salad.

Mary Carozzolo Sorci
John Paul I Lodge #2427

Carne

Geri's Meatballs

This recipe was taught to me by two very dear friends, Catherine and Mafalda Gemmiti. These ladies were regarded as two of the finest cooks in Schenectady, NY.

1 1/2 lbs. ground round	2 tsp. garlic powder
1 1/2 lbs. ground chuck	1 1/2 tsp. salt
6 eggs	1 tsp. freshly ground black pepper
2 cups seasoned Italian bread crumbs	1/3 cup extra virgin olive oil
2/3 cup filtered water	1 tbsp. minced fresh Italian parsley
1/3 cup plus 1 tbsp. grated parmesan cheese	canola oil for frying

Break eggs into a large bowl; whisk until completely combined. Add bread crumbs and mix well with a fork. Gradually add the water; mixing well. Add the cheese and stir in. Add garlic powder; blend in. Stir in the salt and pepper, then add the olive oil and mix well. Blend in the parsley, then add the ground meats and incorporate into the other ingredients until evenly distributed.

Using both hands, roll enough of the meat mixture to form a ball the size of a golf ball. Repeat until all of the mixture is used.

Heat enough canola oil in a large frying pan on medium-high heat. The oil should not be more than halfway up meatballs when several are in the pan - be careful to leave enough space between them for even browning, and ease of rolling them over. When the oil is sufficiently heated, lower the burner setting to medium-low to avoid splattering. To test for doneness, remove and cut one in half.

When cooked, remove each ball with a slotted spoon and drop into a cooking pot of your favorite sauce. Cook meatballs in the sauce for about 1 hour more. Discard the cooking oil. Make at least one day in advance for best flavor.
Yield: approximately 60 meatballs

Geri Mauro
Beaches Lodge #2821

Carne

Grilled Beef Hearts

1 lb. beef hearts, sliced
1/2 tsp. salt
1/2 tsp. pepper

2 tbsp. olive oil
1/2 lemon, 3 wedges

Place meat into a dish with salt and pepper and marinate for 1 hour. Turn every 15 minutes. Put olive oil into a frying pan and cook meat over high heat, 7 to 10 minutes. Turn frequently. Serve nice and hot with lemon wedges, and eat this right away or slices will not be tender. Hurry and enjoy.
Variation: Use veal kidneys.

Dominick Ragosta
Marion County Lodge #2648

Roast Beef Scalzitti

My dad always made this for Italian weddings and other festive occasions. Friends and family always asked him to make the roast beef. When he was asked by one of the neighbors to make the roast beef for a birthday party, he gladly obliged. Unknowingly, he had cooked the roast beef for their own 40th wedding anniversary. Another time, one of our neighbors asked him to cook a roast beef for a "surprise birthday" party. Again, he later found out the "surprise party" was for him and my mom.

5 lbs. rump roast
1 (6 oz.) can tomato sauce,
   or 4 to 5 tomatoes, chopped
1 to 2 tbsp. black pepper

1 to 2 tbsp. rosemary, crushed
1 tbsp. garlic powder
2 beef bouillon cubes
1 to 2 tbsp. chopped garlic cloves

Cook roast for 2 hours, uncovered, at 400 degrees, adding water so it doesn't burn. Let cool at room temperature about 30 minutes. Refrigerate over night.

Cut roast beef into 1/8 inch slices and layer the slices into a large pot. Cover beef completely with water and add remaining ingredients. Cover pot and simmer for 1 1/2 hours.

Gloria Scalzitti Walker
Joseph B. Franzalia Lodge #2422

Carne

Rolled Beef Roman Style

butter
olive oil
3 to 4 carrots, chopped
2 onions, chopped
1/3 cup grated cheese
4 to 6 slices of beef

flour
1/4 cup white wine
1 bay leaf
1 can diced tomatoes
frozen peas, thawed
prosciutto, chopped

In a fry pan, add some olive oil and butter. When hot, add carrots and onions. Sauté for 15 minutes. Put this mixture into a bowl, add cheese and mix. Arrange beef slices on a board and put some carrots, onion and cheese mixture in the center of each slice and roll. Secure with toothpicks. Add more oil and butter to the fry pan. Dredge meat rolls in flour and brown on all sides. Add wine, bay leaf and tomatoes. Cover and simmer on low heat for 30 minutes. Remove meat rolls to a plate. Add peas and prosciutto to sauce and simmer for 5 minutes. Remove toothpicks from meat rolls and pour sauce over meat. Serve with gnocchi and salad.

Mary A. Sorci
John Paul I Lodge #2427

Sicilian Meat Roll

2 eggs, beaten
3/4 cup soft bread crumbs
1/2 cup tomato juice
2 tbsp. chopped parsley
1/2 tsp. crushed oregano
1/4 tsp. salt
1/4 tsp. pepper

1 garlic clove, minced
2 lbs. ground beef
8 thin slices boiled ham
6 oz. shredded mozzarella
3 slices mozzarella,
  halved diagonally

Preheat oven to 350 degrees. Combine eggs, bread crumbs, tomato juice, parsley, oregano, salt, pepper and garlic. Add beef, mix well. On wax paper or aluminum foil, flatten beef mixture into a 10 x 12 inch rectangle. Arrange ham on top of the beef mixture, leaving a small margin around the edges. Sprinkle shredded cheese over the ham. Starting from the short end, carefully roll up the meat mixture, using the paper to lift. Seal the edges and the ends. Place roll, seam side down, into a 9 x 13 inch pan. Bake for 1 1/2 hours. Place the mozzarella slices over the top and bake an additional 5 minutes.

Nancy Baughman
Joseph B. Franzalia Lodge #2422

Carne

Peppers and Sausage Napoletan Style

virgin olive oil
red onions, sliced
red and yellow peppers, sliced
1 cup red wine

Italian sausage
1 can crushed tomatoes
1 tsp. oregano

Sauté red onions in virgin olive oil. Add sliced red and yellow peppers. Add wine and simmer 5 minutes. Add sausage, tomatoes and oregano. Cover and simmer on low heat for 30 minutes. Serve with crusted bread and salad.

Mary A. Sorci
John Paul I Lodge #2427

Spiedini I

3 lbs. sirloin tip roast, cut into
    1/8 inch slices

Stuffing:

1 large onion, finely chopped
1 large onion, parboiled
2 cups plain bread crumbs
1/2 tsp. dried parsley
1 tsp. salt
1/4 tsp. pepper
1/4 tsp. oregano

1 tsp. basil
1 tbsp. pine nuts, crushed
1/4 cup water
butter
ketchup
bay leaves

Preheat oven to 350 degrees. Cut meat into 2 x 3 inch pieces and tenderize with a mallet. Sauté the finely chopped onion. Mix in bread crumbs, parsley, salt, pepper, oregano, basil, pine nuts and water. Quarter the parboiled onion and separate the rings. Place a dab of butter in the center of each piece of meat and add 1 heaping tablespoon of stuffing and 1/2 teaspoon ketchup on the top. Roll meat lengthwise and stick onto a skewer. Alternate meat rolls on skewer with a bay leaf and slice of parboiled onion. Bake for 25 minutes, turning once.

Mary A. Sorci
John Paul I Lodge #2427

Carne

Spiedini II
Spetine: Beef Rolls

3 lbs. eye of round
   (seamless small end)
8 oz. sharp provolone
   cheese (or as needed)
vegetable oil
2 cups seasoned bread crumbs

2 onions, 1/4 inch slices
1 (28 oz.) can whole tomatoes,
   drained and sliced
3 onions, quartered
several bay leaves

Have your butcher slice the eye of round into 1/8 inch thick slices with an electric slicing machine. Ideally, the slices should be 3 inches by 4 inches. If necessary, pound them evenly. Cut provolone cheese into 1 1/2 inches by 1/4 inch by 1/4 inch pieces.

Pour about 1/4 cup vegetable oil into a deep dish. Dip each slice of meat into oil (just one side), then roll in bread crumbs. Place meat onto a work surface, bread crumb side up. Place cheese, onion, and tomato slices on bread crumbs. Roll the stuffed slices of meat, making sure the filling doesn't stick out.

Put meat on skewers, alternating with a quartered onion and a bay leaf. Put 5 spetine to a skewer. When all the spetine are rolled and skewered, sprinkle them with oil and coat them lightly on both sides with bread crumbs.

Barbeque or grill over medium heat for 10 to 15 minutes (or when the cheese oozes out). Yield: 8 skewers of spetine

Note: Spetine can also be made with veal or chicken cutlets.

Marie Gennacci
Sgt. F. M. Bonnano Lodge #2549

Italian Sausage Casserole

4 tbsp. olive oil
8 oz. sausage, without casings
1 cup diced eggplant
1 cup diced zucchini
1 cup diced red or green
   bell pepper
1/4 cup chopped onion
2 cloves garlic, minced
1 (28 oz.) Italian plum tomatoes,
   drained and chopped
2 tbsp. fresh parsley, chopped
2 tbsp. fresh basil, chopped
cayenne or black pepper
2 oz. grated mozzarella cheese

Heat oil in a nonstick pan over medium-low heat. Add sausage and cook for 10 minutes, breaking the meat with a spoon. Remove meat with a slotted spoon and reserve. To the same pan add eggplant, zucchini, bell pepper, onion and garlic. Stir occasionally and cook until vegetables are softened, 10 to 15 minutes. Add the reserved sausage, tomatoes, parsley, basil and cayenne. Simmer an additional 15 minutes over low heat.

Preheat oven to 350 degrees. Spoon mixture into an oven-to-table baking dish and sprinkle with mozzarella cheese. Bake until the cheese melts, about 15 minutes.

Mildred Ajello
John Paul I Lodge #2427

Sausage with Rapini

1 to 2 large bunches rapini
garlic
olive oil
1 lb. sausage
crushed red pepper

Steam rapini with garlic and a small amount of olive oil. Set aside. Fry sausage and break up into small pieces. Mix everything together with red pepper to taste and serve with good crusty Italian bread.

Anne Cristodero
John Paul I Lodge #2427

Carne

Turf and Surf Stew Tuscan Style

1 to 1 1/2 lbs. sweet Italian sausage
3 medium portobello mushrooms, sliced
1/2 cup virgin olive oil
3 garlic cloves, chopped
4 medium potatoes, peeled and sliced
2 carrots, peeled and sliced
2 plum tomatoes, sliced
seasonings: salt, mixed pepper, oregano, parsley
1 leek, chopped
18 to 24 medium shrimp, cleaned and deveined
1/2 cup tomato paste
1 cup white wine

Preheat oven to 350 degrees.

Quickly brown sausage in a fry pan and drain off excess fat. Cut sausages into 1 to 1 1/2 inch pieces.

Inter-mix sausage pieces and mushroom slices in a roasting pan coated with olive oil. Sprinkle with garlic. Layer with potatoes, carrots, and tomatoes. Add seasoning to taste, chopped leeks and shrimp. Mix tomato paste with the wine and pour over meat, shrimp and vegetable mixture. Cover tightly with aluminum foil and bake until potatoes and carrots are soft. Remove foil and bake at 375 degrees for approximately 10 minutes, until the potatoes are slightly brown.

Ann and Ron Albano
Delray Beach Lodge #2719

Cotechino and Lentils

2 lbs. cotechino
1 onion, chopped
1 tbsp. olive oil
2 slices bacon
2 celery stalks, diced
2 cans lentils
parsley flakes

Boil cotechino slowly for 2 hours. Put onion in a pan with oil and brown evenly. Add bacon, celery, drained lentils and 2 cups of the water from the cotechino. Cook slowly for 1/2 hour. When finished, slice the cotechino and place over the lentil mixture in a dish. Garnish with parsley flakes.

Eleanor Renza
Delray Beach Lodge #2719

Carne

My Grandfather's Saltimbocca

My grandfather, Frank Quattrochi, was Venerable in the Amerigo Vespucci Lodge in Danbury, Connecticut for four years. This was his favorite recipe. He once told me that saltimbocca was made famous by the La Tosca Restaurant in Milan. It was prepared in bite-size rolls, and the ladies, who dined there before attending the La Scala opera house, would pick them up with their fingers and drop them into their mouths without smearing their lips. Thus the name, which translates to "jump in the mouth".

8 veal scallops, 1/4 inch thick	**4 tbsp. butter**
salt, pepper, fresh rosemary leaves	**1/3 cup Burgundy wine**
1/4 lb. prosciutto sliced very thin	**1/3 cup sauterne wine**
1/4 lb. mozzarella cheese	**1/4 lb. mushrooms, sliced thin**

Flatten veal as thin as possible to 3 inch squares. Add salt and pepper and place a few rosemary leaves on veal. Cut prosciutto to the same size as veal and place on top. Cover with a slice of cheese and roll tightly. Tie with string or secure with toothpicks.

Brown rolls in butter. Combine wines and add to skillet with mushrooms. Cover, reduce heat, and simmer for about 20 minutes or until tender. Remove string or toothpicks and serve with pan sauce.

John L. Martell
Bradenton Lodge #2782

Carne

Saltimbocca

My mom used to make this as a treat for my father. We all enjoyed this with a loaf of crusty Italian bread.

2 lbs. veal cutlets, thinly sliced
1 tsp. sage
1 pinch of rosemary, chopped
1/4 lb. prosciutto

3 tbsp. butter, separated
salt / pepper
4 slices mozzarella (optional)
3 oz. water

Make cutlets about 6 inches square. Add sage and rosemary. Add a slice of prosciutto to each to cover. Hold together with a toothpick.

Place the cutlets in melted butter, prosciutto side up. Add salt and pepper. Cook both sides over a high heat. Remove the cutlets from the pan. Place mozzarella slices on the prosciutto side of each cutlet and allow to melt for about 4 minutes.

Add water to the pan and scrape. Mix in any remaining butter. Pour this gravy over the saltimbocca and serve hot.

Gerry Paraldi
Charles J. Bonaparte Lodge #2504

Veal Florentine

1/4 cup olive oil
1 onion, sliced
1 garlic clove, crushed
2 lbs. cubed veal steak

1/2 lb. tomatoes, peeled
1/4 cup dry white wine
1 pinch of rosemary
salt / pepper

Heat oil in a large pan. Add onion and sauté for 2 minutes. Add garlic and sauté for 1 minute.

Add meat and brown well on both sides. Add tomatoes, wine, rosemary, and salt and pepper. Cover and cook over low heat for 30 minutes (or until meat is tender).

Lee Teppen
Joseph B. Franzalia Lodge #2422

Veal Marsala

2 lbs. veal cutlets, pounded thin
1/4 cup all-purpose flour
1/2 tsp. salt
1/2 cup butter
2 tbsp. olive oil
3/4 lb. fresh mushrooms, sliced
1/4 cup Marsala wine

Dredge cutlets in flour and salt mixture. Place cutlets on a wire rack for approximately 15 minutes.

In a large skillet melt butter and add oil. Fry cutlets on both sides until brown, and add mushrooms. Reduce heat to low, cover and cook for 10 minutes. Pour Marsala wine into the pan and simmer until veal is tender. Serve immediately.

Tony Celona
John Paul I Lodge #2427

Veal Marsala with Artichoke Hearts

4 veal cutlets, sliced thin
1 egg, beaten
1/2 cup Italian style bread crumbs
4 tbsp. olive oil
1 (6 oz.) jar marinated artichoke hearts
1 small onion, sliced
1/4 lb. mushrooms, sliced
2 tbsp. fresh parsley, chopped
salt / pepper
1 cup beef broth
1/4 to 1/2 cup Marsala dry wine

Preheat oven to 450 degrees. Dip veal into egg and coat both sides with bread crumbs. Sauté until golden brown.

Place cutlets side by side in a baking pan coated with olive oil. On top of cutlets, place artichokes, onion, mushrooms, parsley and salt and pepper. Pour beef broth and Marsala wine over the cutlets. Cover with aluminum foil.

Bake for 15 minutes. Remove foil, reduce heat to 350 degrees and bake for another 15 to 20 minutes.

Donna Burdick, Ft. Walton Beach
mother of Lee Teppen
Joseph B. Franzalia Lodge #2422

Carne

Veal Stew

Veal stew was one of my father's favorite dishes, and he cooked it to perfection.

2 lbs. boneless veal shoulder
1 cup flour
1 tsp. salt
1/2 tsp. white pepper
1 1/2 oz. virgin olive oil
2 garlic cloves, chopped
2 bay leaves
1 cup white wine
3 tbsp. parsley, chopped
1 can crushed tomatoes
2 quarts beef broth
1 lb. mushrooms, sliced
1 cup pearl onions, drained and rinsed
2 tbsp. butter

Preheat oven to 350 degrees.

Remove any fat from the veal. Place the veal lightly in flour, salt and pepper, then brown in olive oil in a large fry pan. Add garlic and sauté to a golden color.

In a dutch oven, add bay leaves, wine, parsley, tomatoes and broth. Place the veal on top and bring to a boil. Place the dutch oven into the preheated oven and cook for 2 hours.

Sauté mushrooms and onions in butter until light brown. When the veal is cooked, put mushrooms and onions in with veal and let stand for 10 to 15 minutes. Serve with rice or egg noodles.

Tina Piasio
Lake Worth/Boynton Beach Lodge #2304

Cotolette di Agnello

2 lbs. lamb cutlets, thinly cut
1 lemon
1 egg, beaten
1 cup bread crumbs

1/2 tsp. salt
1/2 tsp. pepper
1/2 tsp. rosemary, finely chopped
1/2 cup extra virgin olive oil

Squeeze lemon over cutlets and place in the refrigerator for 4 hours. Remove cutlets and drain on a paper towel. Dip cutlets in the beaten egg and then cover with bread crumbs. Place cutlets flat in a tray and sprinkle with salt, pepper, and rosemary. Fry in hot oil until they are a light golden color. Serve nice and hot with lemon slices as a garnish.

Eleanor Renza
Delray Beach Lodge #2719

Lamb Sweetbreads with Prosciutto

1 lb. lamb sweetbreads
2 tbsp. butter
1 pinch of salt
1 pinch of pepper
3 thin slices prosciutto
1 oz. Marsala wine

After soaking sweetbreads in cold water, discard water and refill with fresh water. Boil for 2 minutes. Once again put into cold water, then peel skin. Fry in butter until light brown. Add salt, pepper, prosciutto and Marsala. Cook for 5 minutes. Serve hot with crusty Italian bread.

Lillian Marcelli
Lake Worth/Boynton Beach Lodge #2304

Carne

Lamb's Brains

4 lamb's brains
3 tbsp. olive oil, separated
1 tsp. capers
12 ripe pitted black olives, chopped

1/2 tsp. salt
1/2 tsp. pepper
2 tbsp. bread crumbs

In a pan, cover brains in cold water for 15 minutes. Discard and replace with fresh water, and bring to a boil. Remove brains and rinse in fresh cold water. Dry off. Put 1 1/2 tablespoons olive oil in a low casserole dish and add brains. Cover with capers, olives, salt and pepper. Cover with bread crumbs and add remaining olive oil. Cook in the casserole dish for 15 minutes and enjoy.

Pat Arca
Port Charlotte Lodge #2507

Cappuzelle

4 baby goat heads
6 garlic cloves, chopped
8 stems fresh rosemary
10 tbsp. plain bread crumbs
1/2 cup finely chopped fresh parsley

1 tsp. salt
1 tsp. white pepper
2 cups white wine
1 cup extra virgin olive oil
4 oz. pancetta or bacon

Preheat oven to 450 degrees.

Wash and clean heads. Split them in half.

Mix together garlic, rosemary, bread crumbs, parsley, and salt and pepper. Mix half the wine with half the olive oil and brush over each head. Cover heads with mixture and place bacon on top. Press ingredients gently into the heads and cover brains with heavy aluminum foil so as not to burn.

Bake in a well greased pan for 2 1/2 hours, basting with the remaining oil and wine.

Dennis Piasio
Lake Worth/Boynton Beach Lodge #2304

Coniglio
Rabbit Country-Style

2 lbs. rabbit, cut into pieces
1 carrot, finely chopped
1 small white onion, finely chopped
1 celery stalk, finely chopped
1 tbsp. chopped Italian parsley

1 bay leaf
2 cups dry red wine
salt / pepper
1/4 cup olive oil

Place rabbit pieces into a large deep bowl. Add carrot, onion, celery, parsley and bay leaf. Add wine and mix. Cover and allow to marinate in the refrigerator for 12 hours.

Remove rabbit pieces and vegetables from the marinade with a slotted spoon. Salt and pepper the rabbit pieces. Heat olive oil in a skillet and brown the rabbit on both sides. Add vegetables and a small portion of the wine marinade. Cook covered on medium heat for 1 hour or until tender. If the juices start to dry, add a little more wine marinade. Place cooked rabbit on a serving platter. Serve with rice or polenta.

Tony Celona
John Paul I Lodge #2427

Family Style Oxtail

5 lbs. oxtails
3 bacon strips
1 tbsp. lard
1/2 garlic clove
1 onion, sliced
2 tsp. chopped parsley

1 small celery stalk, sliced
1 carrot, diced
1/2 tsp. salt
1/2 tsp. pepper
2 cups red wine
3 tbsp. tomato paste

Cut oxtails and bacon into small pieces. Melt a small amount of lard to cover the bottom of a pan, and place in the pan the oxtails, bacon, garlic, onion, parsley, celery, carrot and remaining lard. Brown well and add salt, pepper and wine. Cook very slowly until wine evaporates. Mix tomato paste with enough water to cover the oxtails. Cover and cook on low heat about 5 hours.

Eleanor Renza
Delray Beach Lodge #2719

Carne

Delicious Tongue Dinner

This was one of my father's favorites, and the next day we had tongue sandwiches for lunch.

4 to 5 lbs. tongue
2 1/2 quarts water
1/2 garlic clove
1/2 tsp. salt
1/2 tsp. pepper
1 tbsp. butter
1 onion, chopped
1 carrot, chopped

2 strips bacon, cut into pieces
1/4 cup chopped parsley
1 tbsp. flour
1 cup beef broth
1/2 cup wine vinegar
2 bay leaves
2 tbsp. sugar
1 sprig of rosemary

Put tongue into a soup pan with water, garlic, salt and pepper and boil for 2 1/2 hours. Melt butter in a fry pan and add onion, carrot, bacon and parsley. Brown gently over medium heat. Slice tongue about 1/4 inch thick, then sprinkle both sides with flour and brown evenly. Turn over and add beef broth, wine vinegar, bay leaves and sugar. Cook on low heat an additional 15 minutes or until the tongue is nice and tender.

Our Family Style Tripe

My father used to say no one cooks tripe better than him. We all believed him.

1 lb. tripe
1 onion, chopped
4 tbsp. butter, separated
1/4 tsp. salt
1/4 tsp. pepper

2 tbsp. grated mixed parmesan
    and romano cheeses
1 tbsp. chopped parsley
1/4 tsp. cinnamon

Parboil the tripe, then cut into thin strips. Fry onion in 2 tablespoons butter until golden brown. Add the strips of tripe, salt and pepper.

Cook over low heat for 1 hour, turning frequently. Add cheeses, parsley, cinnamon and the remaining butter. Cook another 10 minutes.

Anthony Forgione
Lake Worth/Boynton Beach Lodge #2304

Stufato di Trippa
Stewed Tripe: Grandma's Recipe

2 lbs. honeycomb tripe
3 tsp. salt, approximately
1/4 cup olive oil
4 garlic cloves
1 medium onion
1 tsp. oregano
4 celery stalks,
    chopped in 1 inch chunks
1 large bell pepper, cut in strips
salt / pepper
4 large tomatoes, chopped
    or 1 large can
1/2 lb. small white onions
1/8 tsp. crushed red pepper
1 tsp. sugar

Follow instructions carefully:

Wash tripe thoroughly. Place in a large pot with 3 to 4 quarts salted water. Cover and boil tripe 2 1/2 to 3 hours. Remove and rinse tripe in cold water. Slice into 3/4 inch wide strips, then cut into 2 inch pieces.

In a large skillet simmer garlic, onion and oregano in olive oil for 5 minutes. Add tripe, celery, bell pepper and salt and pepper. Simmer for 10 to 15 minutes.

Add tomatoes, white onions, crushed red pepper and sugar. Simmer for 45 minutes.

Test the tripe. It should be chewy like soft gristle. Serves 6 to 8.

Margaret Scarfia
John Paul I Lodge #2427

Pollo

Braised Turkey Wings

4 turkey wings, cut in two, tips removed
3 tbsp. butter
1 onion, sliced
2 carrots, cut into julienne strips
2 celery stalks, cut into julienne strips
2 to 3 sprigs parsley
12 garlic cloves, peeled
1 cup dry white wine
2 tbsp. tomato paste
1 tsp. rosemary
salt / freshly ground pepper

Preheat oven to 350 degrees. Heat butter in an oven-proof casserole dish and add onion, carrots, celery and parsley. Let them wilt a bit and then toss in garlic cloves. Add wine, tomato paste, rosemary, and salt and pepper to taste.

Arrange turkey wings on top of the vegetables. Cover and bake for 1 1/2 hours or until tender. Remove cover during the last 20 minutes so the wings brown nicely. Serves 4.

Mary Sorci
John Paul I Lodge #2427

Chicken Fra Diavolo

This is my grandmother Maria Quattrocchi's recipe. The only change I made is adding garlic. My grandmother was a rare Italian who didn't use garlic, and yet her food was always the best.

1 frying chicken, cut in pieces
4 tbsp. butter
2 tbsp. olive oil
4 green onions, in 1/2 inch slices
1 garlic clove, crushed
salt
1/3 cup good red wine
2 small red chili peppers, finely crushed
1/2 cup tomato sauce (preferably homemade)

Heat butter and oil in a skillet and brown chicken pieces. Add onion, garlic and salt. When all the chicken is browned, add wine and chili peppers. When wine is almost absorbed, add tomato sauce, blend well, cover and simmer 45 to 60 minutes or until tender.

Susan Kardos
Bradenton Lodge #2782

Chicken alla Ischia

4 chicken breasts, halved to make 8 thin slices
1/2 cup melted butter
1 cup seasoned bread crumbs
8 thin slices prosciutto
8 slices mozzarella cheese

Preheat oven to 350 degrees. Dip the chicken breasts in melted butter, then into bread crumbs. Lay breasts flat and place 1 slice prosciutto and 1 slice mozzarella on each breast. Roll breasts and secure with toothpicks. Place rolls in a greased baking dish and bake for 30 minutes. *Note: The breasts come out moist and tasty.*

Ann DeMarco
John Paul I Lodge #2427

Chicken with Artichokes

4 chicken cutlets
1/2 tsp. black pepper
2 tbsp. flour
1 tbsp. butter
1/2 cup pancetta, diced
1/2 cup onion, diced
1 (10 oz.) bag fresh spinach
1/2 lb. mushrooms, sliced
3 tbsp. Marsala wine
1 cup heavy whipping cream
1/2 cup marinara sauce
1 pkg. frozen artichoke hearts
1/2 lb. prepared tortellini or spaghetti, cooked as directed

Sprinkle chicken with pepper and coat with flour. Melt butter in a 12 inch non-stick fry pan over medium heat. Add chicken and cook 4 minutes per side or until golden. Remove chicken from pan and set aside.

In the same pan add pancetta and onions. Cook and stir frequently until onions are golden and pancetta is crisp, about 3 minutes. Add spinach and mushrooms. Cook for 3 minutes, until spinach is wilted. Add Marsala and bring to a boil. Stir in cream, marinara sauce and artichokes. Reduce heat and simmer for about 7 minutes. Return chicken to pan and cover. Cook 2 minutes more or until chicken is heated. Stir in pasta. Serves 4.

Terry Albanese
Boca Raton, FL

Pollo

Chicken Piccata

4 boneless, skinless chicken breasts, cut in half
1 egg, beaten
3 tbsp. lemon juice, divided
1/4 cup flour
1/8 tsp. garlic powder
1/8 tsp. paprika
1/4 cup butter or margarine
2 tsp. chicken flavored bouillon (or 2 cubes)
1/2 cup boiling water

Beat egg with 1 tablespoon lemon juice. Combine flour, garlic powder, and paprika. Dip chicken into egg mixture and then into flour mixture. Melt butter (or margarine) in a skillet and sauté chicken until brown. Dissolve bouillon in water. Add bouillon and 2 tablespoons lemon juice to skillet. Simmer 20 minutes, or until chicken is tender. Garnish as desired.

Ann DeMarco
John Paul I Lodge #2427

Chicken Cacciatore

4 tbsp. olive oil
3 lbs. chicken, cut into pieces
2 garlic cloves, minced
1 onion, chopped
basil
2 bay leaves
1 tsp. rosemary
1/2 tsp. oregano
2 (14 oz.) cans chopped tomatoes
1/3 cup wine
1/4 tsp. sugar
salt / pepper
2 cups mushrooms, sliced

Heat oil in a large frying pan and brown the chicken pieces. Add garlic, onion, basil, bay leaves, rosemary and oregano. Sauté slowly for about 5 minutes, then add the chopped tomatoes, wine and sugar. Add salt and pepper to taste. Cook slowly for about 20 minutes, then add the mushrooms. If you desire pasta, cook some angel hair and place on a platter. Pour chicken and sauce over the pasta. Add grated cheese on top, if you like.

Jean D'Antonio Fineberg
John Paul I Lodge #2427

Pollo

Chicken with Prosciutto and Tomatoes over Polenta

4 to 6 chicken thighs, skinned
1/4 tsp. salt, divided
1/4 tsp. black pepper
1/2 cup flour
2 tsp. olive oil
1/2 cup dry white wine
2/3 cup yellow cornmeal
2 cups water
1 cup tomatoes, peeled, seeded, and chopped
1 tsp. fresh lemon juice
2 slices prosciutto or ham, cut into very thin strips (1/4 cup)
1/2 tsp. sage (optional)

Sprinkle chicken with salt and pepper. Place flour in a shallow dish and dredge chicken. Heat oil in a nonstick skillet over medium-high heat. Add chicken and cook 4 minutes on each side. Add wine and cover. Reduce heat and simmer for 20 minutes or until meat thermometer reads 180 degrees.

Place the cornmeal and 1/8 teaspoon salt in a 1 quart casserole dish. Gradually add water while stirring until blended. Cover and microwave on high for 12 minutes, stirring every 3 minutes. Let stand while covered for 5 minutes.

Remove chicken from pan. Add tomatoes to pan and cook 1 minute. Stir in the lemon juice and prosciutto. Spoon polenta onto plates and top with chicken and sauce.

Pauline P. Parker
Joseph B. Franzalia Lodge #2422

Pollo

Chicken In Sauce

1 chicken, cut up
1/4 cup olive oil
3 medium onions, diced
4 garlic cloves, chopped
1 tsp. salt
2 tbsp. oregano

2 bay leaves
1 tsp. sugar
1/2 cup cooked mushrooms
2 large cans tomato puree
2 cans tomato paste

In a large pot, brown the chicken in olive oil. After browning, remove the chicken from the pot. Add onions and garlic to the pot and cook until golden brown. Add the remaining ingredients, and bring the mixture to a boil. Put the browned chicken pieces into the sauce and simmer for 2 hours, but do not let the chicken fall apart.

Rosemary Coronato
Sgt. F. M. Bonnano Lodge #2549

Chicken and Sausage Scarpariello

3 lbs. hot or sweet Italian sausage
3 lbs. boneless, skinless chicken breasts
1/2 cup olive oil
garlic
2 medium onions, sliced

2 lbs. green and red peppers, sliced
1/2 tsp. oregano
salt / pepper
1 small bottle sliced hot cherry peppers, with juice

Grill sausage and chicken breasts on a barbeque grill or broil in the oven until only partially cooked.

In a large skillet heat olive oil and sauté garlic, onions, bell peppers, oregano, and salt and pepper until partially cooked. Cut sausage and chicken into bite size pieces and combine with bell peppers and onions. Add hot peppers and juice. Stir and continue to cook 10 to 15 minutes until chicken is fork tender. Serves 8 to 12.

Helen Santoro
Joseph B. Franzalia Lodge #2422

Pollo

Chicken with Sun-Dried Tomatoes and Artichokes

- 4 boneless, skinless chicken breast halves
- 1/8 tsp. salt
- 1/4 cup all-purpose flour
- 1/3 cup white wine
- 1 (13 3/4 oz.) can low sodium chicken broth
- 1 1/2 tsp. cornstarch
- 1 (6 oz.) jar marinated artichoke hearts, drained
- 8 oil packed sun-dried tomatoes, drained
- 1/4 cup fresh parsley, chopped
- fresh ground pepper

Salt chicken and coat with flour, shaking off excess flour. Heat some oil in a large skillet. Add chicken and cook for 3 to 4 minutes per side, turning once until chicken is no longer pink in the center. Add wine to the skillet and cook for 30 seconds. Remove the chicken and cover to keep warm.

Mix chicken broth with cornstarch. Add broth mixture, artichokes and tomatoes to the skillet and bring to a boil. Stir and continue to boil for 4 to 5 minutes until liquid reduces to a sauce-like consistency. To serve, pour sauce over chicken and sprinkle with parsley and pepper.

Barbara Hoff, Plano, TX
daughter-in-law of Pauline Parker
Joseph B. Franzalia Lodge #2422

Pheasant with Cream

My grandfather brought this recipe from the old country and used to brag how good it was.

- 1 pheasant
- 4 tbsp. butter
- 1 medium onion, chopped
- 1 tsp. salt
- 1/2 tsp. pepper
- 1/2 tsp. sage
- 1 1/2 cups heavy cream
- 1 tbsp. lemon juice

Place pheasant in a dutch oven with butter, onion, salt, pepper and sage. Slowly cook and brown nice and easy on all sides for 2 1/2 hours. Add cream and continue to baste while cooking another 30 minutes. Before serving, add lemon juice and mix well. Serve hot.

Anthony Forgione
Lake Worth/Boynton Beach Lodge #2304

Pollo

Sticky Garlic Skewers

3 garlic cloves, crushed
2 tbsp. honey
4 tbsp. tomato sauce or crushed tomatoes
2 tsp. hot pepper sauce
salt / pepper
3 boneless, skinless chicken breasts, cut into thin strips
10 to 12 bamboo skewers

Preheat outdoor grill to high or oven to broil. Soak skewers in water for 15 minutes. In a glass bowl, combine well the garlic, honey, tomato sauce, pepper sauce, salt, pepper and chicken. Marinate 20 to 30 minutes (or overnight).

Thread marinated chicken strips onto skewers. Cook on the grill for 5 to 7 minutes. If broiling indoors, place chicken on a foil lined baking sheet and broil for 6 to 8 minutes, turning often, until well browned and cooked through. Serve with wine, an antipasto salad, and top off with sherbet for a great summer treat! Serves 4.

Irene Lamano
St. Cloud/Kissimmee Lodge #2731

Chicken Francese

2 to 4 chicken breasts, boneless, skinless
flour
2 eggs, beaten
olive oil
4 oz. butter
1/2 cup water
lemon slices
seasonings: black pepper, garlic powder, parsley flakes, rosemary

Pound chicken breasts with mallet. Heat the oil in a frying pan. Place chicken in the flour, coating both sides, then dip in the beaten eggs, coating both sides. Put the chicken into the frying pan, flipping pieces when golden on one side and cooking until golden on the second side.

In a separate pan, melt the butter, place the fried chicken in the pan, add the water and bring to a boil for 1 minute. Turn chicken over and place a small slice of lemon on top. Add seasonings and you're ready to eat.

Otto Ottaviano
Il Fiore d'Italia #2811

Pollo alla Bolognese

4 large boned chicken breasts,
    sliced in half (8 halves)
salt / pepper
flour
3 tbsp. olive oil
2 tbsp. butter

8 thin slices prosciutto,
    2 x 4 inches
8 thin slices provolone,
    2 x 4 inches
4 tsp. grated romano cheese
1/2 cup chicken stock

Lay chicken breasts on wax paper, cover with another sheet of wax paper, and pound with a mallet to flatten. Season with salt and pepper; dip in flour and shake off excess.

Heat oil and butter in a large skillet over medium heat. Add chicken and brown until a light golden color, 3 to 4 pieces at a time. Transfer chicken to a shallow 9 x 13 inch baking pan and place a slice of prosciutto and a slice of cheese on each piece. Sprinkle with grated cheese and dribble chicken stock over top.

Bake uncovered in a 350 degree oven for 10 to 15 minutes, or until the cheese is melted and lightly browned.

Marie Caponero
John Paul I Lodge #2427

Pesce

Acciughe Marinate Napoletana
Marinated Raw Anchovies

Origin: My cousin, Fiorella Giuliani, Battapaglia, Italy.

1/2 lb. fresh anchovies or small
    sardines, 3 inches long
white vinegar
salt

2 tbsp. chopped parsley
2 garlic cloves, minced
crushed red pepper flakes
olive oil

Wash anchovies. Remove spine, clean and wash. Lay flat and pat dry with a paper towel. Place anchovy fillets in a single layer in a glass baking dish. Cover fillets with white vinegar. Sprinkle with salt and marinate for 1 hour. Drain vinegar and pat fillets dry with a paper towel. Sprinkle with parsley, garlic and hot pepper flakes. Lightly cover with olive oil. Can be refrigerated for one week. Serve with bruschetta.

Rose Marie Boniello
Sgt. F. M. Bonnano Lodge #2549

Anguilla I
Baked Eel

2 lbs. large size eel
1/2 cup olive oil
2 tbsp. wine vinegar
3 bay leaves

1 tsp. salt
1/2 tsp. pepper
1 tbsp. bread crumbs

Preheat oven to 350 degrees. Skin eel and cut into 3 to 4 inch pieces. Mix cut eel with oil, vinegar, bay leaves, salt, pepper and bread crumbs. Let mixture marinate for 3 to 4 hours. Turn often.

Put eel pieces in a greased baking dish with a small bay leaf on the top.

Bake in the oven for 40 to 50 minutes. Use remaining marinade and turn often.

Dennis Piasio
Lake Worth/Boynton Beach Lodge #2304

Anguilla II
Fried Eel

3 to 4 lbs. eel, cut in 2 inch pieces
1 cup flour
1 cup olive oil

salt / pepper
1 lemon, quartered

Mix eel pieces in flour and fry in hot olive oil for 15 to 20 minutes each side, until both sides are brown.

Remove and drain on paper towels. Sprinkle with salt and pepper to taste. Place lemon quarters on the side.

Dennis Piasio
Lake Worth/Boynton Beach Lodge #2304

Fish with Tomato Sauce

2 lbs. swordfish or tuna,
  cut 1/2 inch thick
2 tbsp. olive oil
1 garlic clove, minced
4 cups tomato sauce

1 tbsp. fresh parsley, minced
salt / pepper
1/4 cup chopped basil
1 1/4 cups red wine

Preheat oven to 450 degrees. Oil a baking dish. Place the fish in a single layer and brush with oil. Sprinkle with garlic and basil, add the wine, and cover the fish with tomato sauce. Top with parsley, salt and pepper. Cover with foil and bake in the oven for 20 minutes, until fish flakes easily. Serve immediately.

Sam Pittaro
Delray Beach Lodge #2719

Pesce

Buridda Genovese

My father used to enjoy making this during Lent.

1 1/2 to 2 lbs. mackerel
3/4 cup olive oil, divided
2 onions, thinly sliced
8 fresh clams, shelled
1 to 2 tbsp. chopped parsley
1/2 tsp. salt
1/2 tsp. pepper
1/2 cup white wine
1 small can tomatoes

Preheat oven to 350 degrees. Wash and dry fish and cut into 2 inch slices. Put 1/2 cup olive oil into a casserole dish with half of the fish slices. Cover the fish with half of the onions. Add clams, parsley, salt and pepper. Add remaining fish slices and remaining onions. Cover with remaining oil, wine and tomatoes.

Bake in the oven for about 1 hour or until wine evaporates.

Dennis Piasio
Lake Worth/Boynton Beach Lodge #2304

Calamari con Pomodoro
Squid with Tomatoes

2 lbs. squid
4 tbsp. olive oil
2 garlic cloves
salt / pepper
1 pinch of oregano
1/2 cup dry sherry
1 cup solid-pack tomatoes
1 tsp. parsley chopped

Have squids thoroughly cleaned. Cut into small pieces. Wash well.

Pour olive oil in a saucepan and heat. Brown garlic for about 3 minutes. Add squid and cover. Sauté for 10 minutes. Add salt, pepper, oregano and sherry. Cook for 10 minutes over low heat. Add tomatoes and parsley, and cover. Cook for 15 minutes or until tender. Serve very hot on toast. Serves 4 to 6.

Lois M. DeMaio
John Paul I Lodge #2427

Calamari Imbottiti
Stuffed Squid

8 small squid

Buy the squid thoroughly cleaned, with the eyes, outside skin and intestines removed, heads and tentacles cut off. Wash well and drain.

Stuffing:

- 1 small onion, chopped
- 1 1/2 cups bread crumbs
- 1 tsp. minced parsley
- 2 tbsp. grated parmesan cheese
- salt / pepper
- 1 egg, well beaten

Combine remaining ingredients and fill the cavity in each squid with stuffing. Sew squid closed or fasten with toothpicks. Set aside.

Sauce:

- 5 tbsp. olive oil
- 2 garlic cloves, minced
- 1 large can crushed tomatoes
- 1 tbsp. capers
- salt / pepper

Brown the garlic in oil. Add tomatoes, capers, salt and pepper. Simmer for 19 minutes. Place squid in pan and cook for 30 to 35 minutes.

Serve whole with sauce over pasta.

Ann DeMarco
John Paul I Lodge #2427

Pesce

Calamari Ripieni
Stuffed Squid

Origin: Cannizzaro Family Fish Market, Humbolt St., Brooklyn, NY. This recipe was a must on Christmas Eve, served with pepper biscotti, or, for the men, linguine.

2 lbs. squid, cleaned	1 tbsp. parsley, minced
1/2 lb. shrimp, shelled	1 tsp. salt
1 cup plain bread crumbs	1/2 tsp. black pepper
3 garlic cloves, minced	1 tbsp. olive oil
1 tbsp. grated cheese	marinara sauce

Mix shrimp, bread crumbs, garlic, cheese, parsley, salt, pepper and oil together. Fill squid 3/4 full and fasten with a toothpick. Put filled squid in a large sauté pan with a tight lid. Cook on very low heat, and check within minutes. Be sure pan has water or squid juices. Remove squid from pan. It does not have to be fully cooked. Place squid in a marinara sauce and cook until squid is done, not more than 30 minutes. The longer you cook squid, the tougher it becomes.

Elinore Marie Scafiddi
Mike Accardi Lodge #2441

Grilled Calamari

2 lbs. squid	1/2 tsp. salt
2 tbsp. olive oil	1/2 tsp. pepper

Preheat outdoor grill. Remove squid head and skin, and clean thoroughly. Cut squid into pieces. Put squid into a dish with oil, salt and pepper, and marinate for about an hour. Turn every 15 minutes. Remove and drain into a cup.

Put squid onto the hot grill and cook for 20 minutes on each side, while brushing with the oil.

Dennis Piasio
Lake Worth/Boynton Beach Lodge #2304

Calamari Ripieni al Forno
Baked Stuffed Squid

2 lbs. squid, preferably small

Clean squid. Chop fins and tentacles, and set aside for the stuffing. Preheat oven to 375 degrees.

Stuffing:

1 cup course bread crumbs	2 tbsp. capers
1/2 small onion, chopped	2 slices hard salami, diced
2 garlic cloves, chopped	1/4 cup black olives, chopped
1 egg, hard boiled, chopped	salt / pepper
1 egg, well beaten	

Combine all stuffing ingredients, plus chopped fins and tentacles, in a bowl. Mix well. Stuff squid 3/4 full and secure with a toothpick. Set aside.

Sauce:

1/4 cup olive oil	1 handful of fresh basil
2 garlic cloves, chopped	1/4 cup dry red wine
1 (28 oz.) can crushed tomatoes	salt / pepper

Sauté garlic in olive oil. Add tomatoes. Raise heat and add basil. When bubbling, add wine and stir. Reduce heat and simmer 30 minutes. Add salt and pepper to taste.

Pour half of the sauce into a baking dish. Lay in stuffed squid. Pour the remaining sauce over squid. Cover the dish with aluminum foil and bake in the oven for 15 minutes. Remove the foil and baste squid gently. Continue to bake for 10 minutes.

Serve with fresh parsley and lemon wedges. Serves 6.

Margaret Scarfia
John Paul I Lodge #2427

Pesce

Calamari Salad

2 lbs. squid, cleaned
1/4 cup white wine
1/4 tsp. salt
fresh ground pepper

2 whole garlic cloves
1/4 tsp. crushed red pepper
1 bay leaf
4 parsley sprigs

Dressing:

2 tbsp. garlic cloves, finely chopped
3 tbsp. finely chopped parsley
2 tbsp. lemon juice

1 tbsp. red wine vinegar
1/4 cup olive oil
1/2 cup chopped red onion

Cut squid into bite size pieces (include tentacles). Put squid into a small pot and add wine, then add water to cover. Add salt, pepper, garlic, crushed red pepper, bay leaf and parsley sprigs. Cover and bring to a boil. Cook for 1 minute. Drain and chill in a bowl.

When ready to serve, mix together the dressing ingredients, toss and serve. Serves 4.

Mary Sorci
John Paul I Lodge #2427

Clam Cakes

1 cup fresh clams, chopped
2 cups flour
2 tbsp. baking powder
1 tsp. salt

2 eggs
1/2 cup clam broth
1/2 cup milk

Mix all ingredients in a mixing bowl. In a pan with hot cooking oil, drop the mixture by the tablespoon into the hot oil to deep fry.

Ann DeMarco
John Paul I Lodge #2427

Pesce

Clams Casino

5 slices bacon
24 cherrystone clams, washed shelled (reserve shells)
1/4 tsp. oregano
1 celery stalk, chopped
1 garlic clove, chopped
1 red pepper, chopped
1 small onion, chopped
1 parsley sprig, chopped and
3 tbsp. parmesan cheese
1/2 glass white wine
1 pinch of black pepper
1/4 cup ground mixed nuts
1/2 cup bread crumbs

Preheat oven to 400 degrees. Fry bacon until crisp. Remove from pan and allow to cool. Sauté clams for 1 to 2 minutes in the bacon fat. Crumble bacon and add to clams, along with the remaining ingredients, except for bread crumbs and nuts. Cook for 8 minutes. Cool for a few minutes, and add bread crumbs and nuts.

Stuff the clam shells and place on a cookie sheet. Bake in the oven for 8 to 10 minutes or until the topping is a light golden, crusty brown.

Paulette Lombino, Ontario, NY
daughter of Pauline Parker
Joseph B. Franzalia Lodge #2422

Crab Crostini

8 oz. crab meat
1/2 cup chopped red bell pepper
2 tbsp. + 2 tsp. reduced calorie mayonnaise
2 tsp. chopped fresh parsley
1 tbsp. fresh chives
Italian bread, cut into 16 slices

Preheat oven to broil. Line the broiler pan with foil. In a bowl combine all ingredients (except bread) and mix well. Spread 1 tablespoon of the crab mixture onto each slice of bread.

Place bread onto broiler pan and broil 4 inches from the heat for 5 to 6 minutes or until lightly browned. *Note:* To save time, the mixture can be prepared ahead of time and refrigerated until needed.

Ann DeMarco
John Paul I Lodge #2427

Pesce

Granchi Marinara
Crab Mariner's Style

1/4 cup olive oil
2 garlic cloves, minced
1/2 cup chopped green onions
1 (28 oz.) can crushed tomatoes
3 to 4 fresh basil leaves

salt / pepper
1/4 cup dry white wine
1 lb. crab, cooked and flaked
2 tsp. parsley
1 lb. vermicelli pasta
grated romano cheese

Heat oil, and add garlic and onion. Cook for 3 to 5 minutes. Add tomatoes and bring to a boil. Add basil, salt and pepper, and simmer 30 minutes. Add wine and simmer for 10 minutes. Add crab meat and parsley. Stir gently.

Boil vermicelli according to package directions and drain thoroughly. Mix crab meat sauce into the pasta, sprinkle with grated cheese and serve. Serves 6 to 8.

Margaret Scarfia
John Paul I Lodge #2427

Quick Skillet Crab Cover

I was to leave to watch the sun go down at Siesta Beach with a friend. He brought the wine and I drummed this up quickly – really great! I would like to hand this recipe down to my daughter Bonnie who loves to cook and my daughter-in-law Tracy who is an excellent cook. I hope that my two granddaughters Cheyenne and Kaitland take up cooking and try Nana's recipe.

1 pkg. imitation crab meat
pesto sauce

red wine
1 pkg. vegetable-filled ravioli
olive oil

Dice up crab meat, place in a skillet on low heat. Stir in 3 to 4 large tablespoons pesto sauce and just a splash of red wine, and cook. Cook ravioli in a separate pan, adding 1 teaspoon olive oil to the boiling water. Cook for 6 minutes and drain. Place crab meat and sauce over ravioli and serve.

April Strouse
Societa d'Italia Lodge #2698

Shrimp with Arugula Sauce

6 cups water
2 tbsp. white vinegar
2 lbs. shrimp (about 40)
1 1/2 cups packed arugula
1 tsp. sea salt
2 cups extra virgin olive oil
1 red pepper, diced

In a large pot, boil water with the vinegar. Add shrimp and cook 3 to 4 minutes until shells turn red. Cool, peel and devein the shrimp.

Put the arugula and salt into a food processor or blender. Pulse to purée. With the motor running slowly, add the olive oil. Pulse until smooth.

Arrange 5 to 6 shrimp on plates and sprinkle with diced red pepper. Drizzle arugula sauce over shrimp. Serve with lemon wedges and crusty bread.

Sam Pittaro
Delray Beach Lodge #2719

Marinated Shrimp

1 (12 oz.) pkg. frozen shrimp, ready-to-cook
¼ cup olive oil
2 tbsp. lemon juice
1 tbsp. chopped parsley
1/2 tsp. salt
1 garlic clove, crushed

Cook shrimp according to package directions. Plunge shrimp into cold water. If necessary, devein with a sharp, pointed knife. Rinse in cold water; drain.

In a medium bowl combine shrimp with remaining ingredients.

Cover and refrigerate for 6 to 8 hours. Stir occasionally.

Congetta Leccese
John Paul I Lodge #2427

Pesce

Insalata di Gamberi
Shrimp Salad

2 lbs. medium shrimp
1/4 cup olive oil
2 tbsp. chopped parsley
2 tbsp. wine vinegar, or juice of 1 lemon
salt / pepper

Boil shrimp in salted water for 5 minutes until pink. Cool, drain, shell and devein. In a salad bowl, toss shrimp with remaining ingredients. Serve hot or cold.

Ann DeMarco
John Paul I Lodge #2427

Mullet with Prosciutto

1 lemon
3 lbs. mullet
1/2 cup olive oil, divided
1/2 tsp. salt
1/2 tsp. pepper
1/4 tsp. sage
1/2 cup bread crumbs
8 thin slices prosciutto

Preheat oven to 375 degrees. Squeeze juice from lemon.

Remove heads from fish, slit sides of fish and remove the bones. Cut each into 6 to 8 pieces. Combine 1/4 cup olive oil, lemon juice, salt, pepper and sage. Marinate fish in mixture for 2 1/2 hours.

Drain fish and mix with bread crumbs. Put remaining olive oil into a large baking dish and place fish in one layer with a slice of prosciutto in each slit. Pour marinade over fish and prosciutto, and bake in the oven for 25 minutes.

Dennis Piasio
Lake Worth/Boynton Beach Lodge #2304

Pesce Oreganata
Baked Fish Oregano

1 1/2 to 2 lbs. of fish (cod, halibut, turbot, striped bass)
3 tbsp. olive oil
1 tbsp. unsalted butter (optional)
3 garlic cloves, pressed or minced
1/2 tsp. salt
1/2 cup white wine
2 tbsp. finely chopped parsley
1 tsp. oregano
1/2 tsp. dried basil
salt / pepper

Preheat oven to 350 degrees. Place fish in a baking dish to hold fillets in a single layer.

Sauté garlic in heated oil (and butter) until lightly browned. Add wine, parsley, oregano and basil. Cook for 3 to 4 minutes. Pour mixture over fish.

Bake for 15 minutes, until fish is cooked thoroughly. Add salt and pepper to taste. Garnish with parsley and lemon slices.

Margaret Scarfia
John Paul I Lodge #2427

Porgy with Peas

1 small onion, sliced
2 tbsp. olive oil
1 tsp. chopped parsley
1/2 tsp. salt
1/2 tsp. pepper
1 tbsp. tomato sauce
2 lbs. fresh peas
2 1/2 to 3 lbs. porgy

Brown the onion in olive oil, then add parsley, salt, pepper, tomato sauce and peas. Add water to cover the peas and cook slowly until the peas are a little soft. Add the fish pieces and cook slowly, about 20 minutes.

Tina Piasio
Lake Worth/Boynton Beach Lodge #2304

Pesce

Pesce Spada alla Gliotta
Swordfish Messina Style

My father, a native of Messina, used to make this every summer when swordfish was in season. Now the fish is available all year 'round, so I make it several times throughout the year.

1 can tomato paste
2 large cans plum tomatoes, strained (squeeze out pulp and juice)
1 small onion, chopped
6 garlic cloves, whole or sliced
olive oil
4 celery ribs, diced
1 small jar capers, rinsed
20 Italian green olives, pitted
salt / pepper
2 lbs. swordfish, cut into serving pieces
linguine

Combine tomato paste with tomatoes until smooth; set aside. Sauté onion and garlic in olive oil over medium heat. Add celery, capers and olives. Cook for about 2 minutes. Add tomato mixture, salt, pepper and water (if needed). Cook for 20 minutes until celery is almost done.

Add fish and cook for 20 to 30 minutes. Remove fish to a serving dish. Add water to sauce if needed. Pour sauce over cooked linguine.

Jean Lisi Sferlazza
Marion County Lodge #2648

Pesce

Rice with Mussels, Carrots and Peas

I developed this recipe to have a "meal in one dish". Sometimes I vary the ingredients and use clams or shrimp instead of the mussels.

2 to 3 lbs. fresh mussels	1 1/2 cups uncooked rice
1 cup water	3 cups water
1/3 cup olive oil	1 (10 oz.) pkg. frozen peas,
1 large onion, chopped	defrosted and drained
2 garlic cloves, chopped	grated parmesan cheese
2 small carrots, cleaned and cubed	crushed red pepper (optional)
1/4 cup water	

Wash mussels and put into a pot. Add 1 cup water and steam until the mussels open. Discard any that do not open. Remove mussels from shells and reserve mussels and liquid. You may prepare the mussels 1 or 2 days ahead and keep in the refrigerator.

Sauté onion and garlic in oil until tender. Add carrots, 1/4 cup water and reserved liquid from the mussels. Do not add mussels yet. Cover the pan and cook about 5 minutes, or until carrots are just tender.

Cook rice in the 3 cups of water about 15 minutes, or until rice is just cooked. Drain the rice and add to the onion, garlic and carrots mixture. Add peas and mussels and mix together.

Serve as a main dish, or side dish, with grated cheese and, if desired, crushed red pepper. Serves 6.

Ralph Borriello
submitted by Nancy DeGregory
Sgt. F. M. Bonnano Lodge #2549

Pesce

Mussels Marinara

This also serves as an excellent appetizer.

2 tbsp. olive oil
1 medium onion, chopped
2 cloves garlic, crushed
1 large can crushed tomatoes
   or 1 large can whole, peeled tomatoes, broken up
1/2 cup dry white wine
1/2 tsp. salt
1/3 cup chopped fresh parsley
4 doz. (2 lbs.) mussels
1/4 tsp. red pepper flakes

In a saucepan heat olive oil and sauté onion and garlic for 3 minutes. Pour in tomatoes, wine, salt and parsley. Cover and simmer 15 minutes.

Scrub mussels under cold, running water; remove and discard beards, then drain. Add mussels to sauce and steam until mussels open, 5 to 10 minutes. Discard garlic and any unopened mussels. Add hot pepper flakes. Serve in soup bowls with crusty bread or over spaghetti.

Marie Caponero
John Paul I Lodge #2427

Baked Sardines

2 lbs. fresh sardines
1/2 tsp. salt
1/2 tsp. pepper
1/2 tsp. rosemary
1/2 cup olive oil
1/2 cup bread crumbs

Preheat oven to 375 degrees. Clean sardines and remove heads. Marinate in a dish with salt, pepper, rosemary and olive oil for 2 hours. Roll sardines in bread crumbs, put in a well oiled baking dish and pour marinade on top. Bake in the oven for 20 minutes.

Dennis Piasio
Lake Worth/Boynton Beach Lodge #2304

Sardines with Tomato Sauce

2 lbs. fresh sardines
1/2 tsp. salt
1/2 tsp. pepper
1 tbsp. chopped parsley
1/2 tsp. oregano
1 small can tomatoes
1/2 cup olive oil, divided

In a well oiled skillet, put in sardines and sprinkle them with salt, pepper, parsley and oregano.

Hand crush tomatoes and pour on top of the sardines. Add remaining oil and cook on high heat for 4 minutes. Turn sardines and cook another 5 to 6 minutes.

Dennis Piasio
Lake Worth/Boynton Beach Lodge #2304

Scungilli Chowder

4 scungilli
1/4 lb. salt pork, diced
2 garlic cloves
1 onion
1 celery stalk, minced
salt / pepper
1/4 tsp. thyme
1 bay leaf
1/2 tsp. oregano
2 cups canned tomatoes
2 cups diced potatoes
2 sweet peppers, chopped
tomato juice (optional)
sherry

Soak scungilli in salted water for 30 minutes. Drain and pound to tenderize.

Fry the salt pork until crisp. Remove it from the fat and sauté garlic, onion and celery in the pork fat. Add the scungilli, salt, pepper, thyme, bay leaf and oregano. Cover mixture with water and simmer for 2 1/2 hours until scungilli is tender.

Add the tomatoes, potatoes and peppers. Add more tomato juice or water if necessary for a sloshy consistency. Cook until vegetables are tender.

Add some sherry to taste. Serve with Italian bread and salad.

Mary Sorci
John Paul I Lodge #2427

Pesce

Seafood alla Corsetti
Sautéed Seafood and Vegetables

3 tbsp. olive oil	1 small can tuna in oil
2 large red peppers, cut bite size	1 large garlic clove, minced
1 lb. large whole scallops	salt / pepper
1 lb. large whole shrimp	1 tbsp. chopped parsley
1 large sweet onion, wedged	2 large tomatoes, wedged

Put oil in a large fry pan and sauté red peppers. Set aside. Do the same to the scallops and shrimp and set aside. Repeat for onion and set aside.

Cook tuna, garlic, salt, pepper and parsley for 2 to 3 minutes. Return red peppers, scallops, shrimp and onion to the pan. Add tomatoes and cook for 2 to 3 minutes or until warm. Enjoy. Serves 4.

Al Corsetti
John Paul I Lodge #2427

Steamed Cod

My mother Sabastiannina Marinaccio Carozzolo of Acadia, Italy made this as one of her Christmas Eve dishes.

olive oil	fresh bread crumbs
celery stalks	salt / pepper
cod fish	1/4 cup water

In a pot put some oil, lay some celery stalks on top. Put in some cod fish, fresh bread crumbs, salt and pepper. Add another layer of celery, cod fish, bread crumbs, salt and pepper. Add water and sprinkle some oil over top. Cover and simmer for 45 minutes.

Mary Carozzolo Sorci
John Paul I Lodge #2427

Seafood and Eggplant Casserole

2 eggplants, peeled and diced
1 tbsp. salt
1/4 cup olive oil
4 celery stalks, diced
1 onion, diced
1 red pepper, diced
1 green pepper, diced
2 garlic cloves, chopped

1/2 tsp. Tabasco sauce
1 lb. crab meat
1/2 lb. shrimp, peeled and diced
1/4 cup crumbled cracker crumbs
1/4 cup cheese
2 eggs
seasoned bread crumbs

Preheat oven to 350 degrees. Put eggplant in a pot and add water to cover. Add salt, cover pot and boil for 5 minutes. Drain well.

Heat the oil in a sauté pan, and add celery, onion, peppers, garlic and Tabasco sauce. Simmer for 15 minutes. Add the crab meat, shrimp, cracker crumbs, cheese and eggs. Put mixture into a baking dish. Sprinkle seasoned bread crumbs on top. Bake in the oven for 40 minutes.

Mary Sorci
John Paul I Lodge #2427

White Clam Sauce

1/2 stick margarine
1/4 cup olive oil
2 garlic cloves, chopped
4 heaping tbsp. flour
juice from 1/2 lemon

1 (8 oz.) bottle clam juice
2 cans chopped clams
   (reserve liquid)
1 can Progresso white clam sauce
1 tsp. chopped parsley

In a skillet melt margarine and add oil. Add garlic and simmer lightly. Add flour, lemon juice and clam juice (the bottle and the reserved liquid from chopped clams).

When the mixture is at the right consistency, add the clams and the can of clam sauce. Bring to a boil and remove from heat. Add chopped parsley.

Dolly Flaver, Rome, NY
sister-in-law of Pauline Parker
Joseph B. Franzalia Lodge #2422

Pesce

Grilled Butterfish

This, in addition to a nice mixed salad, is great!

3 lbs. butterfish
1/4 cup olive oil
1/2 tsp. salt
1/2 tsp. pepper
3 to 4 tsp. lemon juice, freshly squeezed

Clean, wash and dry fish. Place into a deep dish with olive oil, salt, pepper and lemon juice. Marinate for 1 1/2 hours. Preheat outdoor grill.

Cook on the grill for 15 minutes on each side. Brush the marinade on both sides a few times during cooking.

Dennis Piasio
Lake Worth/Boynton Beach Lodge #2304

Fish Salad - Three Fishes

This salad is not just for Christmas Eve anymore. It is a must to start the dinner for all family get-togethers.

2 lbs. squid, cleaned and cut into rings
2 lbs. shrimp, cleaned and peeled
2 lbs. scungilli or conch
6 lemons, squeezed
8 garlic cloves, finely diced
1/2 tsp. oregano
1 cup olive oil
2 cups finely chopped celery
salt / pepper
crushed red pepper flakes (optional)
6 tbsp. minced parsley
1 lemon, sliced

In a saucepan, bring lightly salted water to a boil. Add the squid rings and tentacles and boil for 2 to 3 minutes. Repeat the same procedure for shrimp and scungilli.

Chop up tentacles and triangular fins. Cool and put in a bowl with all remaining ingredients (except parsley and sliced lemon). Mix well and refrigerate at least 12 to 24 hours. Serve on a platter with sliced lemons and sprinkle with parsley.

Elinore Marie Scafiddi
Mike Accardi Lodge #2441

Pesce

Personal Recipes:

Pesce

Personal Recipes:

Contorni e Insalate

Venice Lodge 2747
Venice

Hollywood Commonwealth Lodge 2761
Hollywood

Celebration Lodge 2777
Celebration

St. Augustine Lodge 2780
St. Augustine

Bradenton Lodge 2782
Bradenton

Artichoke and Green Bean Romano

1/4 cup olive oil
2/3 cup onion, finely chopped
1 clove garlic, minced
1/2 cup Italian bread crumbs
1 (14 oz.) can artichoke hearts,
   drained and quartered
1 lb. fresh green beans,
   cooked and drained
1/2 cup grated romano cheese
salt / pepper

In a large skillet heat the olive oil and sauté the onions and garlic until transparent. Stir in the bread crumbs, blending well to absorb. Add the artichoke hearts, green beans, and romano cheese. Combine thoroughly but gently.

Heat slowly to soften the cheese. Season with salt and pepper to taste.

Lisa Pawlak
Cary, NC

Artichokes, Prosciutto and Parmigiano

I remember my grandfather making this dish on a special holiday when the whole family of aunts, uncles and cousins got together.

15 artichoke hearts, fresh
   or frozen
3 tbsp. butter
15 slices prosciutto
1 oz. fresh lemon juice
6 oz. parmesan or romano
   cheese shavings

Sauté artichoke hearts in butter until all sides are browned lightly. Remove and drain on paper towels. Wrap prosciutto slices around the artichokes and place on a serving tray. Sprinkle lemon juice over all and top with cheese.

Anthony Forgione
Lake Worth/Boynton Beach Lodge #2304

Insalate e Contorni

Stuffed Artichokes I

4 artichokes
3 sprigs parsley, chopped
2 cloves garlic, minced
1/4 cup seasoned bread crumbs

3 tbsp. black olives, chopped
1 tbsp. capers
salt / pepper
olive oil

Using scissors, remove tough outer leaves from base of artichokes. Remove the sharp tips of top leaves. With a spoon scoop out the center. Remove, peel and chop the stems. Place in a mixing bowl and set aside.

Wash artichokes well in salted water. Turn upside down to drain. Add parsley, garlic, bread crumbs, olives and capers to the chopped stems. Mix well and set aside.

Salt the artichokes between the leaves. Stuff the center of each with an equal portion of the stuffing. Place stuffed artichokes in a 6 quart pot. Slowly add 2 inches of salted water to bottom of pot. Sprinkle tops of artichokes with olive oil. Bring to a boil. Lower the heat to a simmer and cover until leaves easily pull away; about 40 minutes.

Ann DeMarco
John Paul I Lodge #2427

Asparagi alla Parmigiana
Asparagus with Parmigiana

2 lbs. asparagus
4 tbsp. butter, melted
1/4 cup olive oil

1 cup grated parmesan cheese
1/2 lemon
salt / pepper

Wash the asparagus. Snap off and discard the tough bottom part of the stalks. Steam the asparagus until almost done. Drain and reserve. Arrange the asparagus on a baking sheet and pour the melted butter and olive oil over top. Sprinkle with cheese. Bake uncovered in a 450 degree oven for 5 minutes or until the cheese melts. Remove from the oven and squeeze lemon juice over the top. Sprinkle with salt and pepper. Serve hot.

Margaret Scarfia
John Paul I Lodge #2427

Insalate e Contorni

Stuffed Artichokes II

4 artichokes
1 loaf hardened Italian bread
1 1/2 cups tomato sauce
4 tbsp. grating cheese

2 tbsp. parsley, minced
salt / pepper
2 cloves garlic, minced
olive oil

Rinse artichokes. Remove tough outer leaves and leaf tips. Remove stems; peel and set aside. Boil artichokes for 10 minutes. Drain and set aside. Chop stems and set aside.

Soak bread with water until soft. Squeeze out water until bread is almost dry. Place in a mixing bowl and add tomato sauce, cheese, parsley, salt and pepper. Set aside.

Using a small frying pan slowly sauté the garlic in olive oil until soft. Add the reserved stems and sauté until tender. Add to the bread mixture.

Place the stuffing between the leaves of the drained artichokes. Place artichokes in a baking pan with about 1 inch of water. Sprinkle tops with olive oil. Cover and bake at 350 degrees for 1 hour. Uncover and bake for another 30 minutes.

Barbara Amoroso
Rome, NY

Artichoke and Chickpea Salad

1 small jar marinated artichokes, undrained
1 small jar red marinated peppers, drained

1 can chickpeas, drained
1/8 tsp. oregano
salt / pepper

Mix all ingredients together. Add some olive oil, if desired. Serve at room temperature.

Celia Flaver
Syracuse, NY

Insalate e Contorni

Butter Bean Sauté

1 (15 oz.) can butter beans
1 tbsp. olive oil
1 small onion, chopped
2 cloves garlic, minced
1 zucchini, about 6 oz., cut in 3/4 inch pieces
1 tsp. sugar
2 tbsp. lemon juice
1 tsp. grated lemon zest
1/2 tsp. salt
1/8 tsp. cayenne pepper
1 jar roasted red peppers, drained, cut in 1/2 inch strips
2 tbsp. chopped parsley

Set aside 2 tablespoons liquid from the can of beans. Drain and rinse beans; set aside. Heat oil in a skillet over medium-high heat. Add onion and garlic, and cook about 4 minutes until softened. Stir in zucchini and sugar, and cook 6 to 7 minutes until onion is lightly browned. Stir in lemon juice, zest, salt, cayenne and reserved bean liquid. Cook for 30 seconds. Stir in pepper strips and reserved beans, and cook until beans are heated through. Remove from heat and stir in parsley.

Ann DeMarco
John Paul I Lodge #2427

Bean Salad

1 (15 oz.) can cannellini beans, drained and rinsed
1/4 lb. soppressata or Genoa salami, diced

Dressing:

1/3 cup red wine vinegar
1/2 tsp. crushed red pepper
2 tbsp. fresh parsley, thyme, and oregano
1 1/2 tsp. Dijon mustard
salt / pepper
2/3 cup extra virgin olive oil

Mix beans and diced meat in a bowl and toss to mix. In a food processor place the remaining ingredients except olive oil. Pulse to blend on slow speed. Slowly add oil; pulse until smooth. Pour over the bean mixture and mix well. Let stand for 2 to 3 hours at room temperature before serving.

Sam Pittaro
Delray Beach Lodge #2719

Insalate e Contorni

Insalata di Fagiolini
String Bean Salad

1 lb. string beans
1/4 cup olive oil

6 tbsp. wine vinegar
salt / pepper

Wash the string beans. Remove ends and strings. Steam the beans in a small amount of lightly salted water until tender. Do not overcook. Drain, cool and set aside.

In a serving bowl, whisk together the oil, vinegar, salt and pepper. Add the cooled string beans and toss to coat. Serve chilled.

Ann DeMarco
John Paul I Lodge #2427

Sedano e Ceci Stufato
Boiled Celery and Chickpeas

This was a favorite dish served on Friday nights.

1 lb. celery, 9 to 10 ribs
3 to 4 tbsp. olive oil
1 large onion, chopped
2 to 3 large garlic cloves, minced
2 tbsp. tomato paste

1 1/2 to 2 cups chicken broth
1/4 tsp. chopped rosemary
salt / pepper
1 (16 oz.) can chickpeas
2 tbsp. chopped parsley

Wash celery and peel to remove strings. Cut in 2 to 3 inch pieces. Heat oil over medium heat and sauté onions until light brown. Add garlic and sauté for 1 to 2 minutes more.

Stir tomato paste into broth and add to onion mixture. Add rosemary, salt and pepper. Bring to a boil. Add celery and cover. Simmer over low heat until celery is tender, about 20 minutes. Add chickpeas and heat through. Add 1 tablespoon parsley, season to taste, and add remaining parsley over top. Use as a main course with crunchy Italian bread. *Variation:* Replace tomato paste with 1/4 cup puree.

Insalate e Contorni

Vascotti and Beans

1 cup dry pinto or kidney beans
6 cups water
salt
Vascotti (or other stale bread), broken into pieces

olive oil
1 to 2 garlic cloves, peeled and sliced
red pepper flakes

Sort beans and soak in water overnight. Drain before cooking. Cook beans in 6 cups salted water until tender. Do not drain cooking liquid.

Place bread pieces in a serving dish, drizzle olive oil over the bread, then sprinkle garlic and red pepper flakes on top. Measure out 3/4 cup beans and liquid and pour over the bread. Allow beans to soften the bread and serve.

Nancy Borriello
submitted by Nancy DeGregory
Sgt. F. M. Bonanno Lodge #2549

Red Bean Salad

My mom showed me how to do this many years ago, and we are still enjoying this dish.

1 large can kidney beans
3 celery stalks, diced
1 small onion, finely chopped
1 clove garlic, finely chopped
2 anchovy fillets, diced
1/2 tbsp. salt

1/2 cup olive oil
1 small can tuna pieces
1/2 cup wine vinegar
1 tbsp. parsley
1/2 tbsp. basil
1/2 tbsp. pepper

Drain and rinse the beans. Combine all ingredients in a salad bowl and marinate for five hours.

Donna Forgione
Lake Worth/Boynton Beach Lodge #2304

Insalate e Contorni

Broccoli Rabe with Sausage

1 full bunch broccoli rabe
1 lb. Italian sausage,
   cut in small pieces
1/2 lb. mushrooms, sliced
2 cloves garlic, chopped
4 tbsp. olive oil
4 extra large eggs
1 cup mozzarella, shredded
crushed red pepper

Wash broccoli rabe thoroughly. Cut into 2 inch pieces, discarding rough ends. Place in a large pot of salted boiling water for 3 minutes. Drain and set aside.

In a large frying pan sauté sausage until brown. Add mushrooms and garlic and sauté 4 minutes or until mushrooms are browned. Add olive oil and reserved broccoli rabe. Sauté 2 minutes.

Beat eggs very well and add to the pan. Cover and cook over medium heat until done. Sprinkle with mozzarella and red pepper. Serves 4.

Lois DeMaio

Broccoli Rabe with Mushrooms

1 large bunch broccoli rabe
4 tbsp. olive oil
4 garlic cloves, minced
1 lb. fresh mushrooms, sliced
salt
red pepper flakes
lemon wedges

Separate broccoli rabe; rinse carefully. Remove and discard tough stems. Cut stalks into thirds and drop into rapidly boiling salted water. Lower heat and cook gently 2 to 3 minutes. Do not overcook. Drain, reserving 1 cup of cooking liquid. Set aside.

Heat olive oil in a large sauté pan. Lightly brown the garlic. Add mushrooms and sauté until soft. Add the drained broccoli rabe, salt and red pepper flakes to taste. Add reserved cooking liquid, if desired. Serve with lemon wedges.

Elinore Scafiddi
Mike Accardi Lodge #2441

Insalate e Contorni

Cavolfiore Fritto
Fried Cauliflower

1 head cauliflower
1 cup flour
1 tbsp. cornstarch
1 1/4 tbsp. baking powder
1/2 tsp. salt
1/4 tsp. pepper
2 extra large eggs, well beaten
2 tbsp. olive oil
1/4 cup warm water
canola oil for frying

Rinse the cauliflower and remove the leaves. Lower the cauliflower into a pot of boiling water and boil for 2 to 3 minutes. Drain. Separate the flowerettes and set aside. Combine the dry ingredients and set aside. Combine the eggs, olive oil and water. Whisk into the dry ingredients until smooth.

In a deep fryer, heat cooking oil to 375 degrees. Dip each flowerette into the batter and drop into the hot oil. Fry 4 to 5 minutes until golden brown. Serve hot.

Margaret Scarfia
John Paul I Lodge #2427

Cavolfiore al Forno
Baked Cauliflower

1 medium cauliflower
1 tbsp. olive oil
1/4 cup bread crumbs
1/4 cup grated parmesan cheese
salt / pepper
1/4 cup olive oil

Remove the outer leaves, core and stalk of the cauliflower. Wash and break into flowerettes; cook in a small amount of boiling salted water until done, about 6 minutes. Drain.

Grease the bottom of a baking pan with 1 tablespoon olive oil. Arrange cauliflower on the bottom of the pan. Combine bread crumbs and cheese and sprinkle over the cauliflower. Season with salt and pepper, then drizzle 1/4 cup olive oil over top and bake in a 350 degree oven for 30 minutes. Add 1/4 cup water if the pan becomes dry. Serve hot.

Ann DeMarco
John Paul 1 Lodge #2427

Insalate e Contorni

Cavolfiore alla Scheriffo
Cauliflower Sheriff's Style

A long time ago in Vicenza, Italy, after introducing my future husband to my mother, she invited him to our home for dinner. Because he was American, she wanted to honor him by creating this dish, naming it to honor his country. This dish is special because of what it represents: the love and respect my mother and my husband always had for each other.

1 large cauliflower
2 eggs, beaten
1/2 cup parmesan cheese
1 tsp. nutmeg
salt / pepper

6 slices cooked ham
6 slices Swiss cheese
bread crumbs
2 tbsp. butter

Steam the cauliflower until done, but firm. In a large bowl place coarsely chopped cauliflower, eggs, parmesan cheese, nutmeg, salt and pepper. Mix well to obtain a very coarse mixture.

Coat a medium baking dish with cooking spray and spoon half of the mixture into the dish. Lightly lay the ham slices on top, then the Swiss cheese slices. Spoon the remaining cauliflower mixture into the baking dish, press lightly, and sprinkle bread crumbs on top. Dot with butter.

Bake at 350 degrees for 35 to 40 minutes. The casserole is done when the top is golden brown and a toothpick comes out clean. Serve hot.

Carola Pesce McReynolds
Navarre, FL

Insalate e Contorni

Stuffed Eggplant

1 large eggplant
4 tbsp. olive oil
2 cloves garlic, minced
1 lb. ground beef
1/2 tsp. dried basil

1/2 tsp. dried oregano
1 cup tomato sauce
salt / pepper
1/2 cup bread crumbs
4 tbsp. grated parmesan cheese

Wash and dry the eggplant. Cut in half lengthwise. Remove the pulp, but leave enough along the sides to create a shell. Set aside.

Heat olive oil in a skillet, add the garlic and slowly sauté until soft. Add the ground beef and brown well. Season with the herbs; add the reserved eggplant and tomato sauce and mix well. Cook 10 minutes over medium-high heat.

Remove from heat and skim off any excess oil. Add salt and pepper to taste. Stir in the bread crumbs, and divide the mixture between the reserved shells. Bake until hot throughout and eggplant is soft. Sprinkle with the grated cheese. Serve hot.

Marie Colello
John Paul I Lodge #2427

Grilled Eggplant

1 to 2 large eggplants
olive oil
3 tbsp. parsley, minced

2 to 3 cloves garlic, minced
salt / pepper
hot pepper flakes, optional

Slice unpeeled eggplant into 1/2 inch slices. Place in a single layer on a broiler pan. Brush each slice with olive oil. Grill until light brown. Turn slices, repeat. Remove and layer on a serving platter, sprinkle with parsley, garlic, salt, pepper, and red pepper flakes. Can also be served as an appetizer. *Variation:* A little white vinegar can be added before serving.

Marie Gennacci
Sgt. F. M. Bonnano Lodge #2549

Insalate e Contorni

Eggplant and Polenta Parmigiana

1 large eggplant, cut
   lengthwise in 8 slices
non-stick cooking spray
3 cups marinara sauce

8 oz. shredded mozzarella
1/4 cup grated parmesan cheese
1 (18 oz.) tube polenta, cut
   in 20 slices

Heat oven to 450 degrees. Coat eggplant slices with non-stick spray; spread on a large baking sheet and bake 20 minutes. Reduce oven temperature to 375 degrees. Place 4 eggplant slices in a 9 x 13 inch baking dish. Spread with 1 cup sauce and sprinkle with 2/3 cup mozzarella and 1 tablespoon parmesan cheese. Repeat once. Top with polenta slices, remaining sauce, and cheese. Bake uncovered for 20 minutes or until bubbly and cheese is melted.

Lee Teppen
Joseph B. Franzalia Lodge #2422

Eggplant Lasagna

1 large eggplant, unpeeled
olive oil
marinara sauce

1 lb. mozzarella, grated
1/2 cup grated parmesan cheese
1 pkg. lasagna, cooked al dente

Wash eggplant. Slice into 1/4 inch rounds; pat dry.

Heat olive oil in sauté pan and quickly fry each round. Place on paper towels to drain.

Line the bottom of a lasagna pan with a little marinara sauce. Top with a layer of lasagna, a layer of eggplant, and sprinkle with mozzarella and grated cheese. Continue this pattern of layers until all ingredients are used. Bake at 350 degrees for 20 minutes.

Rose Dolce Daverese

Insalate e Contorni

Eggplant, Prosciutto and Mozzarella Rollups

1 large eggplant
1 1/2 cups flour
3 large eggs, well beaten
1/4 cup olive oil for frying
3 oz. prosciutto thinly sliced
   in 24 portions
1/4 lb. fresh mozzarella, cut
   into 24 strips
salt / pepper

Wash and dry eggplant. Using a sturdy stainless steel knife, slice the eggplant lengthwise into 12 thin strips. Place on a rack and set aside. Place the flour and eggs in separate shallow bowls. Set aside.

Heat the olive oil in a large skillet. Dredge the eggplant in flour and then dip in the egg, allowing the excess to drip off. Fry 2 coated slices at a time in the olive oil over moderate heat until golden brown, about 2 minutes per side. Transfer to paper towels to drain. Continue the process, adding more oil as required. Pre-heat oven to 400 degrees.

Lay the eggplant on a cutting board. Cut in half crosswise. Cover each half with a slice of prosciutto. Place mozzarella at one end, season to taste, roll up tightly, and secure with a toothpick. Transfer to a serving platter.

Anthony Forgione
Lake Worth/Boynton Beach Lodge #2304

Marinated Eggplant

1 eggplant
1 1/2 cups oil
2 small dried chilies
3 garlic cloves, crushed
3 tbsp. vinegar
2 tsp. oregano
1 tbsp. pepper seeds

Slice eggplant 1/8 inch thick. Arrange in layers in a colander, salting each layer. Weight eggplant down for about 1 1/2 hours, then rinse and pat dry. Arrange in layers in a large mouth jar or crock pot. Make a marinade with remaining ingredients. Pour over each eggplant layer. Seal the jar and refrigerate.

Mary Sorci
John Paul I Lodge #2427

Insalate e Contorni

Eggplant Parmigiana

2 large eggplants
2 cups grated parmesan cheese

1/2 lb. sliced mozzarella cheese
salt / pepper

Marinara sauce:

   2 large cans crushed tomatoes
   3 cloves garlic, chopped
   2 tbsp. dried basil

   3 tbsp. chopped fresh parsley
   1/2 tsp. oregano
   6 tbsp. olive oil

Peel eggplants and cut crosswise into 1/2 inch round slices. Layer eggplant in a colander; sprinkle each layer lightly with salt. Let stand about 20 minutes. Pat dry on paper towels to remove extra moisture. Prepare sauce by combining and cooking the ingredients in a saucepan.

Fry eggplants in hot oil until golden brown. Drain on paper towels. In a baking dish, spread a thin layer of sauce, a layer of eggplant, and sprinkle with grated cheese. Repeat layers, starting with sauce. Cover top with slices of mozzarella cheese. Bake at 350 degrees about 20 to 25 minutes.

Jean D'Antonio Fineburg
John Paul I Lodge #2427

Finocchio alla Genovese

1 large fennel bulb
1 large red delicious apple
3 tbsp. Italian style bread crumbs

cinnamon (optional)
1 tbsp. butter

Remove feathery ends of fennel and discard. Slice fennel bulb thinly and cook in lightly salted boiling water until tender, about 15 minutes. Drain and set aside.

Preheat oven to 350 degrees. Peel the apple and slice thinly. Butter the bottom of a 9 inch plate and sprinkle with 1 tablespoon bread crumbs. Layer half of the sliced apples over the bread crumbs. Top with half of the reserved fennel. Repeat layering procedure, ending with bread crumbs. Bake for 25 minutes. Sprinkle with cinnamon, if desired. Dot with butter.

Luisa Mastromarino

Insalate e Contorni

Roasted Eggplant and Bell Pepper Sandwiches

These sandwiches can be served warm or at room temperature and are great for picnics because they don't require refrigeration.

1 medium to large eggplant	2 red bell peppers
olive oil	4 oz. mozzarella cheese,
3 to 4 soft French rolls,	thinly sliced, enough for
4 inches long	2 slices per roll

Remove the stem of the eggplant, then peel and slice diagonally in 1/4 inch slices.

Roast the red peppers on a cookie sheet under the broiler, turning often, for approximately 15 minutes. Place in a plastic bag to steam for 15 minutes, then peel, seed and quarter the peppers.

Sprinkle the eggplant slices with salt on each side and allow to drain on paper towels for 20 minutes. Blot before baking.

Preheat oven to 475 degrees. Coat a baking tray with olive oil and arrange the eggplant in a single layer. Bake until the slices start to char, approximately 6 minutes per side.

Cut rolls in half lengthwise and liberally coat cut sides with olive oil. Layer ingredients on the bottom halves as follows: eggplant, cheese, bell pepper, cheese. Cover with top halves of bread and wrap in foil, then heat individually wrapped sandwiches on a cookie sheet in a warm oven until the cheese melts a little.

Joneanne Venable
Beaches Lodge #2821

Insalate e Contorni

Escarola Imbottita
Stuffed Escarole Leaves

2 heads escarole
1/2 lb. ground beef or
   sweet Italian sausage
6 tbsp. olive oil
4 anchovy fillets, chopped
1 clove garlic, chopped
1 1/2 tbsp. minced parsley

1/2 cup bread crumbs
4 black pitted olives, chopped
4 green pitted olives, chopped
1 tbsp. pine nuts
salt / pepper
3 tbsp. water

Discard any wilted escarole leaves; wash the heads under cold, running water. Allow the heads to soak while other ingredients are being prepared.

Brown meat in the oil over medium heat for 10 minutes, stirring occasionally. If sausage is being used, reduce the oil to 2 tablespoons. Remove meat from the stove, add anchovies if desired, garlic, parsley, bread crumbs, olives, pine nuts if desired, and very little salt and pepper. Mix thoroughly. Divide the mixture into two parts.

Drain the escarole. Push the leaves away from the center, so the head will lie flat. Place the meat mixture in the center; close the leaves lightly with your hands and press together.

Place stuffed escarole heads close together in a frying pan. Sprinkle with remaining oil, if any, then add water and cover tightly. Cook over medium heat until tender, 18 to 20 minutes. Watch carefully and add a little more liquid if necessary. Remove carefully from pan with a spatula and serve immediately.

Ann DeMarco
John Paul I Lodge #2427

Insalate e Contorni

Escarole Parmesan

2 lbs. escarole
olive oil
bread crumbs, mixed with
    parsley and grated cheese
3 cloves garlic, cut fine
1/2 lb. whole milk mozzarella,
    cut in thin pieces
salt / pepper

Cut the escarole in half before boiling. Strain and let cool. Put some olive oil in a 9 x 6 inch glass baking dish, and spread a layer of escarole. Sprinkle a little oil, bread crumbs, garlic, mozzarella, and salt and pepper. Repeat each layer. Bake at 350 degrees for 30 minutes or until it starts to boil. Yield: 8 servings

Christine DeRosa
Societa d'Italia Lodge #2698

Insalata con Olive
Olive Salad

This may be used as an antipasto, salad or condiment with fish and pork. Keeps well in the refrigerator.

1/4 lb. green Italian olives, pitted
1/4 lb. black Italian olives, pitted
5 pickled green peppers, cut in
    eighths
1/2 cup celery, diced
1/4 cup olive oil
1 large onion, sliced
1 tbsp. oregano
1/4 cup wine vinegar
salt / pepper

Combine all ingredients and mix well.

Ann DeMarco
John Paul I Lodge #2427

Insalate e Contorni

Insalata di Uova, Arancia e Patate
Egg, Orange and Sweet Potato Salad

2 lbs. sweet potatoes
1 head romaine lettuce, washed
4 oranges, sliced in rounds
4 hard boiled eggs, chopped
6 walnuts, finely ground
1/2 cup olive oil
3 tbsp. lemon juice
salt

Boil the unpeeled potatoes in lightly salted water. Cook until easily pierced with a knife. Drain, cool slightly, then peel and set aside to cool. Cut into rounds. Set aside.

Line a platter with romaine leaves. Arrange sweet potatoes in overlapping rows over the lettuce. Peel and place the orange slices on the potatoes. Top with chopped egg and walnuts.

Whisk together the oil, lemon juice and salt. Pour over the salad immediately before serving.

Pauline Parker
Joseph B. Franzalia Lodge #2422

Potato Cake

bread crumbs
2 yellow onions, chopped
6 potatoes, cooked and sliced
1/2 cup grated romanocheese
1/2 lb. prosciutto, cut in strips
5 tbsp. olive oil

Preheat oven to 375 degrees. Grease a springform pan, then coat with bread crumbs. Sauté the onions in the olive oil; set aside. Layer the ingredients in the prepared pan in the following order: potatoes, onions, cheese, prosciutto; repeat layers until all ingredients are used. Put 3 tablespoons bread crumbs on top and drizzle with some olive oil. Bake 40 to 45 minutes. Loosen sides if needed and put on a serving plate. Yield: 6 to 8 servings

Pauline Nicolosi
Delray Beach Lodge #2719

Insalate e Contorni

Spinach Cheese Bake

2 tbsp. butter
3 eggs
1 cup flour
1 cup milk
1 tsp. salt
1 tsp. baking powder
2 (10 oz.) pkg. chopped spinach
1 lb. grated cheddar cheese

Preheat oven to 350 degrees. Grease a 9 x 13 inch baking dish with butter. Beat eggs, flour, milk, salt and baking powder in a large bowl. Drain spinach add to egg mixture and mix. Add cheese and mix. Pour into buttered dish.

Bake for 35 minutes; cool for 10 minutes and cut into squares.

Louise Agnetti
Societa d'Italia Lodge #2698

Stuffed Peppers

6 large bell or frying peppers
3 cups stale bread
2 eggs
3/4 cup grated cheese
2 cloves garlic, minced
2 tbsp. parsley, minced
olive oil
1 recipe tomato sauce, heated

Cut the tops from the peppers, remove seeds, rinse and set aside to dry.

Combine the bread, eggs, cheese, garlic and parsley. Divide the mixture into the peppers.

Heat the olive oil and sauté the stuffed peppers. Remove the peppers to a pot and cover with the warm sauce. Simmer for 60 to 90 minutes.

Terri Branciforte
Mike Accardi Lodge #2441

Insalate e Contorni

Tortelloni Salad

Great for Pot Luck dinners or on a hot summer night.

2 lbs. tortelloni
1 small head broccoli
1/4 lb. salami
1/4 lb. ham
1/4 lb. provolone
1 can artichoke hearts
1 can black pitted olives

Dressing:

1 cup olive oil
1 clove garlic, minced
2 tbsp. Dijon mustard
2 tbsp. vinegar

Cook tortelloni, drain and put in a large bowl. Steam the broccoli, cut into bite size pieces. Cut up salami, ham and provolone into bite size pieces. Chop the artichoke hearts. Mix all ingredients with the tortelloni.

Put all dressing ingredients in a blender and mix well. Pour over salad ingredients and mix. Add salt and pepper to taste. Refrigerate to chill. Toss when ready to serve. Yield: 8 to 10 servings

Dorothy Paradiso
Societa d'Italia Lodge #2698

Zucchini Sausage Pie

1 lb. loose Italian sausage
1/2 cup grated mozzarella
1/2 cup grated parmesan
1 quart grated zucchini
2 1/2 cups Bisquick
1/2 cup oil
4 eggs
salt / pepper

Cook the sausage and drain fat. Mix all ingredients in a bowl and pour into a pie dish. Bake in a 350 degree oven for 45 minutes.

Grace Fallacaro
Mike Accardi Lodge #2441

Insalate e Contorni

Zucchini Frittata

1 tbsp. olive oil
1 medium onion, finely chopped
2 cloves garlic, finely minced
1/2 cup green peppers, diced
1 medium zucchini, sliced thin
1 tomato, chopped
6 extra large eggs
1 cup milk
1/4 cup Italian bread crumbs
1 tbsp. oregano, minced
salt / pepper

Heat the olive oil in a 10 inch ovenproof skillet over medium heat. Add the onion, garlic and green peppers. Sauté until tender. Add the zucchini and tomato. Sauté for 5 minutes. Set aside.

Beat the eggs in a large bowl. Add milk and bread crumbs. Stir in oregano, salt and pepper. Pour over vegetables in the skillet. Mix well to be sure vegetables remain well distributed. Cover skillet and cook over medium heat until eggs are set; about 25 minutes. Brown top under broiler for 2 to 3 minutes. Cut into wedges and serve.

Irene Lamano
St. Cloud/Kissimmee Lodge #2731

Zucchini Pie

14 oz. zucchini with flowers
2 large eggs
4 tsp. flour
1/2 cup milk
3 large spring onions, chopped
1/2 clove garlic, minced
4 tsp. parmesan cheese
salt / pepper
olive oil

Finely chop the zucchini; toss with a little salt. Place in strainer and allow to drain for 20 minutes.

Beat together, eggs, flour and milk to form a smooth batter. Pat the zucchini dry. Mix the zucchini, onions, garlic and cheese into the batter and pour into two greased 8 inch baking tins. Sprinkle with a little pepper and several tablespoons of olive oil. Bake in a preheated 425 degree oven, about 30 minutes, until golden brown. Sprinkle with additional parmesan cheese and serve.

Lois DeMaio

Baked Zucchini Gratin

2 lbs. zucchini, shredded
salt / pepper
2 tbsp. olive oil, divided
3 cloves garlic, chopped
1/4 cup parsley, chopped

2 tbsp. chopped basil
2 extra large eggs, beaten
4 tbsp. ricotta cheese
3 tbsp. Italian bread crumbs

In a large bowl combine the zucchini, and salt and pepper. Let stand for 5 minutes. Drain any accumulated water and set aside.

Heat 1 tablespoon olive oil in a large skillet. Add the zucchini and cook until the moisture evaporates. Add the garlic and cook for 5 minutes. Add the parsley and basil. Remove from heat and set aside.

In a large bowl, combine the eggs and ricotta. Stir in the zucchini mixture. Place the ingredients in a lightly oiled one quart baking dish. Top with bread crumbs and 1 tbsp. olive oil. Put into a preheated 400 degree oven. Bake until browned, about 25 minutes.

Irene Lamano
St. Cloud/Kissimmee Lodge #2731

Insalate e Contorni

Condimento per Insalata
Salad Dressing

1 cup olive oil
1/3 cup red wine vinegar
2 tsp. oregano

1/4 tsp. garlic salt
1/4 tsp. onion salt
1/2 tsp. pepper

Combine all ingredients in a pint jar. Shake vigorously with a tight cover. This can be stored without refrigeration.

Margaret Scarfia
John Paul I Lodge #2427

Gorgonzola Salad Dressing

1/4 cup crumbled gorgonzola
   cheese
1 1/2 tsp. Dijon mustard
6 tbsp. extra virgin olive oil

1/8 tsp. salt
1/8 tsp. freshly ground pepper

Put cheese and mustard in a food processor. Blend slowly until smooth, and add olive oil. Mix until well blended; add salt and pepper. Place in refrigerator. Dressing will keep for 2 weeks.

Sam Pittaro
Delray Beach Lodge #2719

Insalate e Contorni

Personal Recipes:

Insalate e Contorni

Personal Recipes:

Dolci e Feste

Clermont Lodge 2784
Clermont

Amici d'Italia Lodge 2791
Jacksonville

Il Fiore d'Italia Lodge 2811
Port Richey

Beaches Lodge 2821
Jacksonville Beach

Madison Lodge 2822
Madison, Georgia

Biscotti Abbruzzese

2 lbs. flour
7 eggs
2 cups sugar
1 cup milk
1 cup vegetable oil

1 large lemon peel, grated
6 level tsp. baking powder
1 egg for egg wash
1/2 cup granulated sugar
cinnamon (optional)

Preheat oven to 350 degrees. In a large bowl add the flour and make a well. Then mix together everything in the following order: eggs, sugar, milk, oil, lemon peel and baking powder. Mix well with hands until smooth. Cover with a towel and let stand for about 20 minutes. Using a teaspoon, spoon dough onto an ungreased cookie sheet. Brush with egg wash and sprinkle with sugar. When ready to bake, raise the oven temperature to 375 degrees. Bake until golden brown. A dusting of cinnamon can be added after the cookies have cooled. Yield: 8 dozen

Lucia Paolucci
Santo Eusanio, L'Aquila, Italia

Cranberry Pistachio Biscotti

1/4 cup light olive oil
3/4 cup white sugar
2 tsp. vanilla extract
1/2 tsp. almond extract
2 eggs

1 3/4 cups all-purpose flour
1/4 tsp. salt
1 tsp. baking powder
1/2 cup dried cranberries
1 1/2 cups pistachio nuts

Preheat oven to 300 degrees. In a large bowl, mix together oil and sugar until well blended. Mix in the vanilla and almond extracts, then beat in the eggs. Combine flour, salt, and baking powder; gradually stir into the egg mixture. Mix in cranberries and nuts by hand. Divide dough in half. Form 2 logs, 12 x 2 inches, on a cookie sheet that has been lined with parchment paper. Dough may be sticky; wet hands with cool water to handle dough more easily. Bake for 35 minutes or until logs are light brown. Remove from oven and set aside to cool for 10 minutes. Reduce oven heat to 275 degrees. Cut logs on the diagonal into 3/4 inch thick slices and return on sides to the cookie sheet. Bake approximately 8 to 10 minutes, or until dry, then cool.

Gloria Walker
Joseph B. Franzalia Lodge #2422

Dolci e Feste: Cookies

Pistachio Biscotti

3 eggs
2 egg yolks
1 tsp. vanilla
zest of 1 lemon

Mix the above ingredients in a mixer at low speed.

1 1/4 cups sugar
2 1/2 cups flour
1 pinch of salt
1 tsp. baking powder
3/4 cup pistachio nuts

Add the first 4 ingredients to the top mixture, mixing well. Add the pistachio nuts. Dough will be stiff. Place on a well-floured board. Knead and add flour to keep the dough firm. Divide into 4 parts and shape into rolls 2 inches wide. Place 2 inches apart on a greased cookie sheet. Bake at 350 degrees for 25 minutes. Cool slightly and while still warm, cut diagonally into bars, about 1 inch wide. Return to a 275 degree oven for 20 minutes on each side. *Note:* You can change nuts to cherries, hazelnuts, apricots or almonds.

Ann DeMarco
John Paul I Lodge #2427

Almond Cookies

4 large egg whites, room temperature
3 1/4 cups sugar
3 1/2 cups unblanched almonds, finely ground
1/4 cup + 1 tbsp. orange juice
1 tbsp. orange zest
confectioners sugar
parchment paper

Heat oven to 300 degrees. Line 2 cookie sheets with buttered parchment paper. In a large bowl beat the egg whites until foamy. Beat in sugar, 1 tablespoon at a time. Then beat until the whites form stiff peaks. Gently fold in ground almonds, orange juice, and orange zest. Using 2 teaspoons against each other, place 1 teaspoon of the batter at a time onto the cookie sheets. Shape into 1 inch ovals, spaced about 2 inches apart. Bake for 20 minutes, until firm to the touch. Cool on the cookie sheets. Remove with a spatula and dust with confectioners sugar.

Sam Pittaro
Delray Beach Lodge #2719

Dolci e Feste: Cookies

Aunt Millie's Anise Cookies

3 1/4 cups flour
1 tsp. baking powder
1 tsp. cream of tartar
1/2 tsp. salt
1/2 lb. margarine or butter

1 1/4 cups sugar
2 eggs
6 tbsp. milk
2 tbsp. anise seeds
confectioners sugar

Mix together the first 4 ingredients in a bowl, and set aside. In a large mixing bowl cream together the margarine (or butter) and sugar until light and fluffy. Add the eggs and milk. Mix well. Add the dry mixture to the creamed mixture and mix well, then add the anise seeds, continuing to mix well. Chill the dough for at least 3 hours.

Preheat oven to 350 degrees. Shape the dough into 1 inch balls and roll in the confectioners sugar. Place on a greased cookie sheet, and bake for 8 minutes or until cookies are golden in color. Cool on a wire rack.

Pauline Nicolosi
Delray Beach Lodge #2719

Funzis Cookies

12 jumbo egg yolks, room
    temperature
1/4 lb. butter, softened
1 lb. flour

1 tbsp. baking powder
1 cup milk
1 cup powdered sugar
lemon juice

Beat the eggs yolks for 15 minutes. Add butter and beat for 1 minute. Work in the flour, then the baking powder and milk. Let batter rest for 1 hour.

Grease and flour a cookie sheet. Using a teaspoon, drop the batter (not too close together) onto the prepared sheet. Bake at 350 degrees until light brown; allow to cool. Combine powdered sugar and lemon juice to make a glaze for the cookies.

Marie M. Colello
John Paul I Lodge #2427

Dolci e Feste: Cookies

Cherry Slices

5 cups flour
1 1/2 cups sugar
2 1/2 tsp. baking powder
1 pinch of salt
1 tsp. almond extract
3/4 cup shortening, melted
1 small bottle maraschino cherries with the juice
1 cup chopped nuts
5 eggs
confectioners sugar, optional

Sift all dry ingredients together. Make a well in the center and add the remaining ingredients, including the liquid from the cherries. Mix well and knead briefly until smooth. Shape into three small rolls and bake at 350 degrees on a greased cookie sheet for 15 to 20 minutes. Glaze, if desired, with confectioners sugar mixed with a small amount of milk.

Ann DeMarco
John Paul I Lodge #2427

Egg Biscuits

3 large eggs
1 cup milk
1 cup vegetable oil
2 tbsp. flavoring (your favorite)
1 1/2 cups sugar
1/2 tsp. salt
5 cups all-purpose flour
5 tsp. baking powder
confectioners sugar

In a bowl add eggs, milk, oil, flavoring, sugar and salt. Mix for about 2 minutes until well blended, then add flour and baking powder. Stir until dough becomes workable by hand. Break off pieces of dough, roll between hands, twist into a knot, or form into desired shapes. Place on an ungreased cookie sheet and egg wash each cookie with separately beaten eggs. Bake at 350 degrees for 8 to 10 minutes or until tops are light brown. Cool cookies and frost.

Frosting: Mix together **warm milk, flavoring and confectioners sugar** to a frosting consistency.

Ann DeMarco
John Paul I Lodge #2427

Dolci e Feste: Cookies

Mama Sacco's Biscotti

10 eggs, beaten
all-purpose flour

In a large mixing bowl, add the flour to the beaten eggs, 2 cups at a time, until the dough is not sticky on your fingers. Take a piece of the dough, roll like a log, about 1 inch around, and twist into a donut shape. Repeat until all of the dough is used up. Lay the formed dough on a tablecloth and let rise for 15 minutes.

Boil water in a large pot. Add the donuts to the boiling water, a few at a time, then remove right away, placing the donuts onto a towel.

Preheat the oven to 350 degrees. Place the donuts on a greased cookie sheet, not too close together. Bake until golden brown, about 10 minutes.

After the donuts have cooled, cut each one into 3 pieces. Place 3 tablespoons of water in a pot to warm, then melt some sugar in the water a little at a time. Place donut pieces in sugar mixture to coat, then put on a cookie sheet to dry.

Martha Fuoco
Delray Beach Lodge #2719

Dolci e Feste: Cookies

Cuccidati
Fig Bars

Filling:

- 1 lb. dates, pitted
- 1 lb. figs
- 1 cup raisins
- 1 cup nuts
- 1 orange
- 1 can crushed pineapple, drained
- 1 tsp. nutmeg
- 1/2 tsp. cinnamon
- 1/2 cup whiskey
- 1/2 cup grape jelly or jam

Dough:

- 1 cup Crisco
- 1/2 cup sugar
- 4 cups flour
- 3 1/2 tsp. baking powder
- 1/2 tsp. baking soda
- 1/2 cup milk
- 3 eggs
- 1 tsp. vanilla

Frosting:

- confectioners sugar
- water
- 1 tsp. vanilla

Grind the filling ingredients together and set aside.

Cream the Crisco and sugar, then add dry ingredients alternately with the milk.

Roll the dough and cut into strips. Lay the filling mixture on center of the strip and seal with dough wrapped over. Cut into desired lengths. Bake at 400 degrees for 15 to 20 minutes. Frost, using confectioners sugar, water and vanilla.

Mary Ann Latona
John Paul I Lodge #2427

Dolci e Feste: Cookies

Italian Fig Bars

This recipe is from my niece, Ann Sorci, in Amhurst, New York.

Dough:

- 3 lbs. flour
- 3 tbsp. baking powder
- 1 lb. sugar
- 1 lb. lard, melted
- 9 eggs, beaten
- zest of 1 orange
- 1/4 cup water or orange juice
- 1 1/2 tbsp. vanilla

Mix all dry ingredients. Add melted shortening and beaten eggs. Add orange zest, juice and vanilla, and mix well. Refrigerate for 1 hour.

Filling:

- 1 1/2 lbs. figs
- 1/2 lb. raisins
- 1/2 lb. brown sugar
- 1/2 lb. dates
- 1 lb. almonds or filberts
- 1 orange
- 1/2 lb. candied citrus fruit
- 2 tsp. cinnamon
- 1 tsp. black pepper
- 2 oz. rum or anise flavoring
- 1 tsp. salt
- 6 oz. Maraschino cherries: drain, reserve liquid, cut up

Frosting:

- 1 1/4 cups confectioners sugar
- juice from 1 orange
- 1 tbsp. butter, softened
- some milk, if needed

Boil the figs and raisins with the brown sugar in 2 cups water for 15 minutes. Save the water. Grind the figs, raisins and dates with nuts and a whole orange. Add citrus fruit, cinnamon, pepper, rum or anise flavoring, salt and cherries. Add reserved liquid from the cherries. This filling is better if made 2 or 3 days ahead and refrigerated. Roll out dough to the thickness of a pie crust. Cut into strips 3 inches wide. Put filling in center and roll dough over it, sealing the edges. Then cut into 2 inch bars or larger. Bake at 375 degrees for 25 minutes. Cool on a rack, then frost by combining the confectioners sugar, orange juice and softened butter. Add a little milk if needed for spreading. *Note:* If you don't like candied citrus fruit, substitute with 1 pound more of the dates.

Mary Sorci
John Paul I Lodge #2427

Dolci e Feste: Cookies

Lemon Drop Cookies

8 cups flour
8 tsp. baking powder
6 eggs
1 1/2 cups sugar

1 cup milk
1 cup vegetable shortening
4 1/2 tbsp. lemon extract

In a large bowl sift together flour and baking powder. In another bowl beat together eggs and sugar. Add milk, vegetable shortening and lemon extract to the egg mixture. Combine wet and dry ingredients into a soft dough, cover the bowl with plastic wrap, and refrigerate for 1 hour.

Remove dough from refrigerator. Preheat oven to 350 degrees. Pinch off small pieces of dough, about 2 tablespoons in size, and roll them into 4 inch long strands, twisting into a knot or circle or any shape you wish. Place the cookies 1 inch apart on an ungreased cookie sheet. Bake for 10 to 12 minutes. Do not allow them to brown.

Icing:

1 box (16 oz.) confectioners sugar

1 dash of milk
4 1/2 tbsp. lemon extract

While cookies cool, combine icing ingredients in a large bowl. Whisk together until smooth. Dip the cooled cookies into icing, and place on a rack until icing hardens.

Christina DeRosa
Societa d'Italia Lodge #2698

Dolci e Feste: Cookies

Italian Molasses Cookies

4 eggs, beaten
1 cup oil
1 small bottle molasses
1 cup sugar
6 cups flour
4 tsp. baking powder
1 tbsp. anise extract
1 pinch of salt
grated orange zest from 2 oranges

Combine eggs, oil, molasses and sugar. Combine flour, baking powder, anise extract and salt. Stir in the orange zest. Dough will be stiff. Place the dough on a well-floured board or tabletop. Knead and add enough flour to keep dough from becoming sticky. Divide into 4 equal parts; shape into rolls that are about 2 to 2 1/2 inches wide. Place 3 inches apart on a greased cookie sheet and bake at 350 degrees for 25 to 30 minutes. Cool slightly and, while still warm, cut diagonally into bars 1 inch wide.

Ann DeMarco
John Paul I Lodge #2427

Pineapple Cookies

1 can crushed pineapple
6 tsp. baking powder
6 cups flour
2 cups sugar
2 cups Crisco
6 eggs
confectioners sugar

Drain the crushed pineapple, reserving the juice. Mix together the baking powder, flour and sugar, then add the remaining ingredients. More flour may be needed (dough will be sticky). Drop onto a cookie sheet, do not make them too big and bake at 350 degrees for 10 to 12 minutes. Make an icing with confectioners sugar and the pineapple juice. Frost when cool.

Mary Ann Latona
John Paul I Lodge #2427

Dolci e Feste: Cookies

Nana's Pastry

2 eggs
3 tbsp. vinegar
2 cups margarine

5 cups flour
1 tsp. salt
lemon preserves,
   or pie or fig filling

Put 1 egg into a 1 cup measuring cup, add the vinegar to the egg and fill the cup with cold water. Beat with a fork. Cut margarine into flour and salt until well blended. Add the egg mixture and mix to form a stiff dough. Divide dough into 2 balls; roll each ball between 2 pieces of wax paper until you make the size of a 1 inch high cookie sheet. Line the bottom and sides of the cookie sheet. Fill with lemon preserves or pie or fig filling. Top with the remaining rolled dough. Prick top with a fork all over the top of the pastry. Egg wash the top with a beaten egg. Bake in a 400 degree oven for about 30 minutes or until golden brown.

Ann DeMarco
John Paul I Lodge #2427

Pepper Biscuits

8 cups flour
2 tsp. salt
2 tbsp. baking powder
1 tsp. black pepper
1 tbsp. fennel seed

1 cup hot water
1 tsp. anise
3 eggs
1 cup oil
1 cup milk

Mix flour, salt, baking powder, black pepper, and fennel seed together. Make a well and add hot water. Do not mix yet. In a separate bowl, mix anise, 2 eggs, oil and milk together, and add to the flour mixture. Now mix together to make a dough. Roll into strips and make a ring-shaped biscuit. Place on a cookie sheet and brush with 1 egg beaten with 2 tablespoons water. Bake at 350 degrees for 20 to 25 minutes or until brown.

Elaine Cerzosimo
St. Cloud/Kissimmee Lodge #2731

Dolci e Feste: Cookies

Durdilla
Italian Christmas Wine Cookie

My recipe for durdilla seems to be very rare, as I have not seen it in any Italian cookbook. It is indeed a tribute to my dear mother, who passed away in October 2000, to have her mother's old recipe included.

8 cups all-purpose flour
1 3/4 tsp. baking powder
4 cups red Burgundy wine
1 pinch of fresh ground
   black pepper

2 cups virgin olive oil
   (yellow, not green)
1/2 gallon vegetable oil
   (omit if using baking method)
2 lbs. honey

Sift flour into a large mixing bowl. Add baking powder and blend well with a wire whisk. Reserve 1 cup of the mixture and set aside. Bring the wine to a boil, add the black pepper and reduce heat to a low boil. Allow the wine to concentrate for 15 minutes, then add olive oil, stirring occasionally, and bring back to a boil. Remove from the heat and allow to cool to room temperature. Using a wooden spoon, add the cooled wine/oil mixture into a bowl containing seven cups of flour. Slowly add the reserved cup of flour to bring the mixture to a hand-working consistency.

Remove dough from the mixing bowl and place on a flat work surface. Knead the dough with fists, folding frequently, until it becomes a uniform wine color. Flatten the dough to 1 1/4 inch thickness, then cut into strips 1 1/4 inch wide. Cut off enough dough to make a ping pong size ball. Roll on a flat surface, in a circular motion with the palm of your hand, then quickly bring closed, straight fingers across the dough ball, pressing down with fingertips to form a large 'gnocchi'. Place on a tray and allow to set at least one hour. Bring the vegetable oil to 350 degrees in a 3 to 4 quart pot. Cook durdillas 25 to 30 minutes. Remove and drain on paper towels. If preferred, the durdillas may be baked in a 350 degree oven for 1 1/2 to 1 3/4 hours. *Note:* With either method, a sample cookie should be cut in half to test for a thoroughly cooked purple center.

In a 3 to 4 quart saucepan heat at least 2 pounds of honey to a simmer. Submerge durillas for at least 5 minutes, frequently moving them with a slotted spoon. Reduce heat if honey starts to foam. Remove durdillas from honey bath and place on a tray to cool. Yield: 44 durdillas

Joseph A Mirabella
La Nuova Sicilia Unita Lodge #1251

Dolci e Feste: Cookies

Mostaccioli

3 beaten eggs
2 cups sugar
1/2 lb. butter or margarine, melted
4 tbsp. cocoa
2 tsp. cinnamon
1 tbsp. almond extract
1 tbsp. orange extract
zest of 1 orange
1/2 cup cold coffee
1 tbsp. baking powder
4 cups flour
1 cup chopped walnuts
1/2 cup raisins

Mix together. Pour the mixture into a greased 15 x 10 inch jellyroll pan. Bake at 325 degrees for 35 to 40 minutes.

Frosting:

4 tbsp. margarine
1 2/3 cups powdered sugar
1/4 tsp. vanilla
1 egg white

Beat together well. Spread on the cooled cake; cut into small squares or diamonds.

Rose Tassone Gombos

Pizzelle

6 eggs
3 1/2 cups flour
1 1/2 cups sugar
1/2 lb. margarine, melted
4 tsp. baking powder
2 tbsp. vanilla or anise extract

For chocolate pizzelle, add:

1/2 cup dry cocoa
1/2 cup sugar
1/2 tsp. baking powder

Add all of the ingredients. Mix until well blended. Then spoon by the teaspoonful onto a hot pizzelle grill.

Ann DeMarco
John Paul I Lodge #2427

Pignoli Cookies

This is a favorite holiday cookie.

2 1/2 cups (13 oz.) blanched almonds
2/3 cup sugar
grated zest of 1 lemon
2 extra large egg whites (or 3 medium)
1/2 tsp. almond extract
1/2 tsp. vanilla extract
70 to 80 whole pine nuts

Preheat oven to 350 degrees. Brush 2 large cookie sheets with oil and line with parchment paper.

In a food processor or blender, process almonds in small batches with 1 tablespoon of sugar until finely ground. Combine almond grounds in a large bowl with the rest of the sugar and the lemon zest.

In a large bowl beat egg whites until stiff (not dry). Add the extracts. Stir egg whites into the almond mixture until well blended.

Roll into 1 inch balls. Put 4 or 5 pine nuts on top of each ball. Bake for 25 to 30 minutes, until lightly browned. Cool slightly and transfer to wire racks. *Variation:* Candied cherries can be substituted for the pine nuts. *Note:* You can bake ahead and freeze in plastic bags for up to 1 month. Yield: 3 dozen cookies

Marie Caponero
John Paul I Lodge #2427

Dolci e Feste: Cookies

Sesame Cookies

2 1/2 cups flour
1 1/4 cups finely ground
   semolina flour
1 tbsp. baking powder
2/3 cup sugar
1/2 cup lard or Crisco

2 large eggs, beaten
zest of 1 lemon
2/3 cup milk
1 egg, beaten with
   1 tbsp. water (egg wash)
2 cups sesame seeds

Preheat oven to 350 degrees. Lightly grease 2 cookie sheets. In a bowl mix the flours and baking powder together. Add sugar and mix, add lard and work into the flour mixture until it resembles coarse corn meal. Add 2 beaten eggs and lemon zest. Add milk, a little at a time. Work the mixture until a ball of dough is formed. Divide dough into 4 pieces. Roll each into a rope 18 inches long and the thickness of your middle finger. Cut into 2 inch long pieces. Dip in egg wash. Roll in sesame seeds and place on cookie sheets about 1 inch apart. Bake for 20 to 25 minutes or until browned. Cool on racks.

Sam Pittaro
Delray Beach Lodge #2719

Thumbprint Cookies

1 1/2 cups margarine or butter
1 3/4 cups sugar
1 egg
1 tsp. vanilla

4 cups flour
1 tsp. baking powder
jam or jelly

Cream margarine or butter with sugar. Add egg and vanilla. Mix the baking powder with flour and add to the creamed mixture. Break small pieces from the dough and form into balls. Set on greased cookie sheets. Make a depression in the center of each ball and fill it with jam or jelly. Bake at 350 degrees for about 15 minutes or until lightly brown.

Ann DeMarco
John Paul I Lodge #2427

Dolci e Feste: Cookies

Tordilli
Italian Honey Cookies

This recipe was given to me by my daughter-in-law Angela, whose grandmother is also named Angela. "Grandmother" Angela Sacco was born in Nocera Torinese, Italy in 1910. She lives by herself in her own home in my hometown of Monessen, PA, where she still cooks and bakes special Italian dishes. My daughter-in-law's mother Lena Mascetta (grandmother Angela's daughter) and her husband Tony live on the same street in Monessen. Lena and her mother make tordilli for all holidays, weddings, baptisms, First Holy Communions and all special occasions. She makes Bill and me feel really special, with a large plate of her special tordilli, whenever we return to Monessen to see our son Robert, daughter-in-law, and their two beautiful sons.

3 large eggs, beaten   **1/3 cup vegetable oil, lukewarm**

Pour oil over eggs and mix. Set aside.

1 tbsp. baking powder   **1 1/2 cups vegetable oil**
3 cups port wine   **1 large jar honey**
flour, up to 4 lbs.

Combine baking powder and port in a pot, boil for 5 minutes, then simmer for 5 minutes. While still warm, pour into the bowl with the egg mixture. Add up to 4 pounds of flour, a little at a time, and mix like bread dough until smooth. Cut into strips like large gnocchi and roll between your fingers just like gnocchi. Fry in vegetable oil a little at a time. Set aside.

Boil 1 tablespoon water in a pan. Add the honey by pouring half the jar into the water at a time to get hot. When honey bubbles at the side of the pot, add some fried dough to coat. Repeat until finished.

Martha Fuoco
Delray Beach Lodge #2719

Dolci e Feste: Cookies

Wine Biscuits I

5 cups flour
5 tsp. baking powder
1 cup sugar
1 tsp. salt

3 eggs
1 cup salad oil
1 cup wine

Mix flour, baking powder, sugar and salt in a large bowl. Make a well in the center and add 2 eggs, oil and wine. Mix all together. Knead well and roll out. Place on a cookie sheet. Before baking, brush tops with egg mixture (1 egg and 2 tablespoons water). Bake at 350 degrees for 20 to 30 minutes.

Elaine Cerzosimo
St. Cloud/Kissimmee Lodge #2731

Wine Biscuits II

1 cup sugar
1 cup vegetable oil
1 cup wine, red or white
4 1/2 cups all-purpose flour

2 tbsp. baking powder
1 tsp. salt
1 egg, beaten

Beat together the sugar, oil, and wine. Combine 3 cups flour, baking powder and salt in a bowl and add the liquids. Mix until dough forms a ball, using the remaining flour as needed to knead dough until it is not sticky. You may even need more flour. Let stand uncovered for 1/2 hour. This is optional. Roll into desired shapes or roll between hands in 2 to 3 inch strips and connect into a donut shape. Place on ungreased cookie sheets. Brush tops with beaten egg. Bake at 375 degrees for 25 to 30 minutes until golden brown. Yield: 3 to 3 1/2 dozen

Anne DeMarco
John Paul I Lodge #2427

Dolci e Feste: Cookies

Personal Recipes:

Dolci e Feste: Cakes

Cheesecake a la Chiyoko

A very light and tasty cheesecake!

Crust ingredients:

- 1 1/2 cups graham cracker crumbs
- 3 tbsp. sugar
- 1/2 tsp. ground cinnamon
- 1/4 cup (1/2 stick) sweet butter, melted

Filling ingredients:

- 3 pkgs. (8 oz. each) cream cheese, room temperature
- 1 1/4 cups sugar
- 6 eggs, separated
- 1 pint sour cream
- 1/3 cup all-purpose flour
- 2 tsp. vanilla
- grated zest of 1 lemon
- juice of 1/2 lemon
- confectioners sugar

Crust: Generously grease a 9 x 3 inch springform pan with butter. Place pan in the center of a 12 inch square of aluminum foil and press foil up around the side of the pan. Combine crust ingredients in a small bowl; mix until well blended. Press 1/4 cup of the crumb mixture into the bottom and side of the pan. Chill the prepared pan while making the filling (reserve remaining crumb mixture for topping).

Filling: With an electric mixer on slow speed, or with a wooden spoon, beat cream cheese in a large bowl until soft. Gradually beat in sugar until light and fluffy. Beat in egg yolks, one at a time, until well blended. Stir in the remaining ingredients except confectioners sugar, and mix until smooth. Beat egg whites until they hold stiff peaks. Fold whites into the cheese mixture, soufflé fashion, until well blended. Pour into the prepared pan. Bake in a moderate 350 degree oven for 1 hour 15 minutes or until top is golden; turn off oven heat and allow the cake to cool in the oven for 1 hour. Remove cake from the oven and cool on a wire rack. Sprinkle remaining crumbs on top. Chill overnight before serving. Dust with confectioners sugar before serving.

Chiyoko and Bill Zuppa
Joseph B. Franzalia Lodge #2422

Dolci e Feste: Cakes

Italian Cheesecake

4 eggs
1 lb. ricotta cheese
1/2 lb. cream cheese
1 1/2 cups sugar
2 tsp. vanilla

1/2 tsp. lemon juice
3 tbsp. cornstarch
3 tbsp. flour
1/4 lb. + 2 tbsp. butter
1 pint sour cream

Beat eggs slightly and set aside. Cream cheeses together with sugar. Add vanilla, lemon juice, cornstarch and flour. Melt butter and add. Add sour cream and then the eggs. Bake in a springform pan at 325 degrees for 1 hour. Shut off oven and leave the cake in the oven for 2 more hours.

Fran Stanco
St. Augustine Lodge #2780

Quick Cheesecake

2 pkgs. Pillsbury Crescent Rolls
2 pkgs. regular cream cheese
3/4 cup sugar

1 tsp. vanilla
1 egg yolk
powdered sugar

Unroll 1 package of the rolls and spread on the bottom of a 9 x 13 inch cookie sheet. Mix cream cheese, sugar, vanilla and egg yolk. Spread the cream cheese mixture on top of rolls. Spread out the second package of rolls and put on top of the cheese mix. Bake at 375 degrees for 20 to 25 minutes. Cool after cooking and sprinkle with powdered sugar. Cut into triangles.

Eleanor Santore
Port Charlotte Lodge #2507

Dolci e Feste: Cakes

Ricotta Cheesecake

This very delicious cake is wonderful for birthdays or special events. It is easy to prepare. Not having a crust really adds to the taste. The recipe was given to me by a student of mine, and I think of her every time I make this dessert.

4 eggs
1 cup sugar
1 tsp. vanilla
1/4 cup flour
3 lbs. ricotta

1/4 to 1/2 cup anise
citron (small jar)
plain bread crumbs
confectioners sugar (optional)

Beat the eggs, then add the sugar a little at a time. Add vanilla and beat again. Gradually add flour, then ricotta cheese. Beat well until smooth. Add anise and citron. Grease a springform pan with butter or margarine and dust with plain bread crumbs. Pour the batter into the pan and place in the oven to cook until the top gets dark, about 30 to 40 minutes. Turn the oven off and leave the cake in for 10 to 15 minutes longer. Remove cake and let sit for 20 to 25 minutes. Dust the top with confectioners sugar if desired.

Terri Branciforte
Mike Accardi Lodge #2441

Chiyoko's Tomato Soup Cake

1/2 cup Crisco
1 cup sugar
1 can tomato soup
2 cups flour

1 tsp. baking soda
2 tsp. baking powder
1 tsp. cinnamon
1 tsp. nutmeg

Mix Crisco and sugar, then add tomato soup. Add all the other ingredients and mix together. Place in a greased loaf pan and bake at 350 degrees for 45 to 50 minutes.

Chiyoko and Bill Zuppa
Joseph B. Franzalia Lodge #2422

Cheese - Raisin Pound Cake

This is my family's favorite.

1 (8 oz.) cream cheese, softened (not fat-free)
2 sticks (1 cup) butter, softened
1 1/2 cups sugar
4 large eggs, room temperature
2 tsp. baking powder
2 tsp. vanilla
1/4 tsp. salt
2 1/4 cups all-purpose flour
1 1/2 cups raisins
confectioners sugar

Heat oven to 325 degrees. Coat a 10 x 4 inch tube pan, with a removable bottom, with nonstick spray. Beat cream cheese and butter with mixer on medium-high speed until well blended, scraping the sides. Gradually add sugar and beat until pale and fluffy, scraping sides often. Reduce the speed to medium and add eggs, one at a time, beating after each. Add baking powder, vanilla and salt, and beat slightly. Using a rubber spatula, fold in flour, 1/2 cup at a time, until blended, then fold in raisins. Pour into the prepared pan. Bake 1 hour or until a wooden pick inserted in center comes out clean. Cool completely in the pan on a wire rack. Run a spatula around the sides of the cake. Invert on a platter and dust with confectioners sugar. Serves 16. *Note:* This recipe freezes well.

Eleanor Santore
Port Charlotte Lodge #2507

Crumb Cake Supreme

3 cups flour
1 cup sugar
1/2 tsp. baking soda
1/2 lb. butter, melted
2 cans pie filling (if apple, add 1 tsp. cinnamon and 1/4 cup sugar)

In a large bowl, mix flour, sugar, baking soda and melted butter together until crumbly. Set aside 1 cup for the topping. Spread the rest on sides and bottom of a greased 9 x 13 inch glass pan, patting lightly. Pour pie filling over the crumbs and spread evenly. Sprinkle reserved topping. Bake at 350 degrees for 50 to 60 minutes.

Louise Agnetti
Societa d'Italia Lodge #2698

Dolci e Feste: Cakes

Cannoli Cake

6 large eggs, separated
1/2 cup sugar
1/4 cup flour
1 tbsp. baking powder
1/2 tsp. salt
1/2 cup sugar
1 tsp. + 1 tsp. + 3/4 tsp. vanilla extract
2 large oranges
2 tbsp. orange flavored liqueur (optional)

1 (32 oz.) container ricotta cheese
1 (8 oz.) pkg. cream cheese, softened
1 cup + 1 3/4 cup confectioners sugar
1/4 cup + 1/3 cup semi-sweet chocolate mini pieces
3 tbsp. butter or margarine, softened
3 tbsp. milk
2 cups heavy cream

In a large bowl with mixer at high speed, beat egg whites until soft peaks form. Beating at high speed gradually sprinkle 1/2 cup sugar, 2 tablespoons at a time, beating well after each addition until the sugar completely dissolves and whites form stiff peaks. Heat oven to 375 degrees.

In a small bowl, with mixer at low speed, beat egg yolks, flour, baking powder, salt, 1/2 cup sugar, 1 teaspoon vanilla and 2 tablespoons water until blended. Gently fold 1/3 beaten egg white mixture into yolk mixture. Then fold yolk mixture into remaining whites. Spoon batter into an ungreased 10 x 3 inch springform pan. Bake for 30 to 35 minutes until cake is golden and top springs back when lightly touched with a finger. Invert cake pan on a wire rack; cool completely.

Grate enough zest from the oranges to measure 2 teaspoons and set aside. Squeeze enough juice from the oranges to measure 1/3 cup (if not using liqueur, increase orange juice to 1/2 cup). Stir orange flavored liqueur into juice and set aside.

In a large bowl with mixer at low speed, beat ricotta cheese, cream cheese, grated orange zest, 1 cup confectioners sugar and 1 teaspoon vanilla until smooth. Stir in 1/4 cup semi-sweet chocolate mini pieces. With a metal spatula gently loosen cake and remove from pan. With a serrated knife, cut the cake horizontally into 2 layers. Brush orange juice mixture evenly over cut side of both layers. Place one cake layer, cut side up, onto the plate. Spoon ricotta cheese filling at center of cake layer. Spread filling to 1/4 inch of rim of cake. Place top

Dolci e Feste: Cakes

layer. In a small bowl with mixer at medium speed, beat butter or margarine, milk, 1 3/4 cup confectioners sugar and 3/4 teaspoon vanilla, beating until smooth. Add more milk if necessary; beat until frosting has an easy spreading consistency.

In a large bowl with mixer at medium speed, beat heavy cream until soft peaks form. Fold the confectioners sugar mixture into whipped cream. Spread frosting over top and sides of cake.

In a 1 quart saucepan over low heat, melt 1/3 cup semi-sweet chocolate mini pieces. Spoon the melted chocolate into a small decorating bag with a small writing tip or use a paper cone with the tip cut to make a 1/8 inch-diameter hole. Pipe the chocolate on top of cake in a spiral design, starting in the center and moving to the edge of cake quickly, before chocolate hardens. With the tip of a toothpick or small knife draw lines in a spoke fashion. Make spokes about 1/2 inch apart around edge of cake. Alternate directions of each spoke. *Note:* For easier cutting, refrigerate the cake for about 3 hours until the filling is firm.

Ann DeMarco
John Paul I Lodge #2427

Italian Rice Cake

This recipe was donated to our original lodge cookbook over 16 years ago by one of our members. We're still enjoying it.

18 eggs
2 1/2 cups sugar
2 tsp. vanilla
1 tsp. salt

2 lbs. ricotta cheese
2 1/2 cups uncooked rice
   (makes 6 cups cooked rice)
1/2 lb. butter

Beat eggs with sugar, vanilla and salt. Add ricotta cheese and mix well. Combine hot rice and butter until butter is melted and rice is well coated. Put rice into egg mixture and mix well. Pour into two 11 x 13 inch pans or one large lasagne pan. Sprinkle with nutmeg. Bake at 350 degrees for 1 hour or until a toothpick comes out clean. Cool and cut into squares.

Marie LoSapio

Dolci e Feste: Cakes

One Step Pound Cake

1 cup (2 sticks) butter, room temperature
2 cups granulated sugar
2 1/4 cups all-purpose flour
1/2 tsp. baking soda
1/2 tsp. salt

1 (8 oz.) container pineapple or orange yogurt
3 eggs
1 tsp. lemon or orange zest
1 tsp. vanilla

Glaze:

1/2 cup confectioners sugar
1 to 2 tbsp. lemon juice

Heat oven to 325 degrees. Grease and flour a 10 inch (12 cup) bundt, tube, or loaf pan. Beat together butter, sugar, flour, baking soda, salt, yogurt, eggs, zest and vanilla at low speed in a large bowl until well blended. Increase speed to medium, beat 3 minutes. Pour into prepared pan.

Bake in the oven for 50 to 60 minutes or until wooden pick inserted in the center comes out clean. Transfer pan to a wire rack and cool 15 minutes. Turn cake out onto the rack to cool completely.

When cake is completely cooled, whisk together confectioners sugar and lemon juice in a small bowl until well blended and smooth. Drizzle over cake. *Note:* To serve, cut the pound cake into thin slices and top with fresh berries, sliced fruit, frozen yogurt or a scoop of sorbet.

Ann DeMarco
John Paul I Lodge #2427

Easy Ricotta Marble Cake

1 marble cake mix
1 (32 oz.) container ricotta
1 cup sugar
4 eggs
1 tsp. vanilla

Prepare the cake mix and pour into an ungreased 9 x 12 inch pan. Set aside.

Preheat oven to 350 degrees. In a large bowl lightly mix (do not beat) the remaining ingredients with a large spoon. Pour the ricotta mixture over the cake mixture. Bake for 1 to 1 1/4 hours until done.

Pauline Nicolosi
Delray Beach Lodge #2719

Spumoni Cake

1 cup margarine (2 sticks)
2 cups sugar
4 eggs
4 cups flour
4 tsp. baking powder
1 (13 oz.) can evaporated milk
2 tsp. vanilla
1/2 cup chopped nuts
3 to 4 drops green food coloring
1/2 tsp. almond extract
1 small jar cherries, drained and chopped
3 to 4 drops red food coloring
2 oz. unsweetened chocolate, melted

Cream margarine and sugar together, add eggs one at a time. Combine flour and baking powder. Add to margarine and sugar, alternating with milk, and mix well. Add vanilla. Mix for about 3 minutes.

Divide the batter into three bowls. First bowl: mix batter with nuts and green food coloring, add almond extract. Second bowl: mix batter with cherries and red food coloring. Third bowl: mix batter with melted chocolate.

Grease and flour a tube pan. Add green batter first, then pink batter, then chocolate batter. Bake in a 350 degree oven for 40 to 60 minutes.

Ann DeMarco
John Paul I Lodge #2427

Dolci e Feste: Cakes

Zuppa Inglese
Italian Rum Cake

1 yellow cake or sponge cake, cut into 4 equal layers
1 cup dark rum
yellow cream (recipe below)
chocolate cream (recipe below)
strawberry filling (or apricot/orange marmalade), as needed
whipped cream, as needed
1 pkg. ladyfingers
1 small jar maraschino cherries

Place the first layer of cake on a large serving platter. Brush the layer with some of the rum. Spread a layer of yellow cream on top of the layer. Place the second layer of cake on top of the first layer. Brush the layer with some of the rum. Spread a layer of chocolate cream on the top. Place the third layer of cake on top of the second layer. Brush the layer with some of the rum. Spread a layer of yellow cream on the top. Place the fourth layer of cake on top of the third layer. Cover with strawberry filling. Cover the entire cake, top and sides, with whipped cream. Press the ladyfingers around the outer side of the entire cake in a vertical fashion. Garnish with cherries.

Yellow cream:

6 egg yolks
1 quart milk
8 tbsp. sugar
8 tbsp. flour
1 pinch of salt
1 grated lemon rind

Chocolate cream:

6 egg yolks
1 quart milk
8 tbsp. sugar
8 tbsp. flour
1 pinch of salt
1 grated lemon rind
2 cubes bittersweet chocolate

Beat the egg yolks thoroughly. In a saucepan, combine the egg yolks, milk, sugar, flour, salt and grated lemon rind. Mix well. Cook over low heat for about 10 minutes or until thick. Do not allow to boil. Remove from heat and cool. If chocolate flavor is desired, repeat the entire process, and melt the bittersweet chocolate in the hot mixture, stirring well.

Ann DeMarco
John Paul I Lodge #2427

Dolci e Feste: Pies

Apple Pie

6 Granny Smith apples
3 tbsp. flour
3/4 cup sugar
1/4 tsp. salt
1/2 tsp. nutmeg

1 tsp. cinnamon
1 cup walnuts
1 pkg. Pillsbury refrigerated
    pie crusts

Heat oven to 425 degrees. Prepare pie crusts as directed. Peel and slice apples. Mix flour, sugar, salt, nutmeg and cinnamon. Add walnuts. Place apples in pie shell. Pour cinnamon mix over the apples. Place second pie crust on top. Brush milk over top of pie, then sprinkle sugar over top. Bake 40 to 45 minutes.

Grace Brooks
Nature Coast Lodge #2502

Peach Ricotta Pie

2 peaches, peeled, halved,
    pitted and sliced
1 cup melba toast crumbs
1/4 cup sugar
2 tbsp. olive oil

1/4 tsp. cinnamon
1 1/2 cups skim ricotta cheese
1/3 cup sugar
1 egg white, lightly beaten
1 cup lowfat peach yogurt

Combine toast crumbs, sugar, olive oil and cinnamon in a medium bowl. Pour into a 9 inch pie pan and press firmly into sides and bottom. Arrange peach slices over crust. In another bowl combine ricotta, sugar, egg white and peach yogurt. Mix with electric mixer until smooth. Pour yogurt mixture over peaches and bake at 350 degrees for 50 minutes. Let stand to cool to room temperature, then refrigerate for 2 hours until well chilled.

Mary Ann Rawdon
St. Augustine Lodge #2780

Dolci e Feste: Pies

Easter Ricotta Pie

Dough:

4 cups flour	1/2 lb. margarine
2 tsp. baking powder	3 egg yolks
3/4 cup sugar	10 tbsp. orange juice

Mix flour, baking powder and sugar in a bowl. Cut margarine into the mixture. Make a well in the mixture, add egg yolks and orange juice. Knead the dough, adding flour a little at a time so it is not sticky. Wrap dough in a towel to rest while you make the filling.

Filling:

3 lb. ricotta cheese	zest of 1 lemon
1 1/2 cups sugar	1 tbsp. cinnamon (optional)
eggs	1/2 cup chocolate chips,
vanilla	(optional)
zest of 1 orange	

Beat ricotta, sugar, eggs and vanilla on medium speed until well blended. Add orange and lemon zests. Sprinkle cinnamon and add chocolate chips, if desired.

Divide the dough into 4 pieces. Roll out 3 pieces of dough and put into 3 pie pans. Add the egg and ricotta mixture to the pans, filling 3/4 full. Roll out and cut the 4th piece into strips to make lattice tops on the pies. In a preheated 350 degree oven, bake 1 to 1 1/2 hours, until tops are light brown and puff up. Remove from oven and let cool. Sprinkle with confectioners sugar if desired. Yield: three 8 inch pies

Pauline Nicolosi
Delray Beach Lodge #2719

Dolci e Feste: Pies

Easter Rice Pie

This recipe was given to me from Auntie Carmella. I have been making it for many years at Eastertime.

1 quart milk
1 cup rice
1 lemon peel
1 orange peel
1 cinnamon stick

Cook milk, rice, lemon peel, orange peel and cinnamon stick in a pot for 20 minutes. Remove pot from the stove, remove cinnamon stick, lemon and orange peels. Reserve the lemon and orange, set aside.

1 cup sugar   **1 stick butter or margarine**

To the rice mixture add the sugar and butter; stir until well blended.

8 eggs, beaten   **1 tsp. vanilla**
1 lb. ricotta

Add eggs, ricotta, vanilla, and the reserved orange and lemon peel (I use half a peel), chopped fine. Grease and flour a 13 x 9 inch glass baking dish. Put the rice mixture in the prepared baking dish and sprinkle with nutmeg. Bake in a 350 degree oven for 30 minutes, until a toothpick in the center comes out clean.

Ann DeMarco
John Paul I Lodge #2427

Dolci e Feste: Pies

Italian Cream Pie

My mother would arise at 6:00 a.m. every Good Friday to make her Easter pies: Ricotta, Rice, Wheat, and Italian Cream. It was a treat that we looked forward to each year.

Crust:

- 3 eggs
- 1/2 cup sugar
- 2 tbsp. shortening
- 2 cups flour
- 2 tsp. baking powder
- 1 tsp. vanilla
- 1 pinch of salt

Mix crust ingredients together and prepare as any pie crust; after rolling out the pie crust, place in a 12 inch pie pan. **Editor's note:** Bake in a preheated 325 degree oven for approximately 15 minutes.

Pudding Filling:

- 3 egg yolks
- 1 cup sugar
- 1 cup flour
- 1 quart milk
- 1 tbsp. vanilla or lemon extract
- 1/2 cup cocoa

Put all filling ingredients, except for the cocoa, into a saucepan. Over medium heat, stir until thickened. Remove some of this pudding into a small bowl. Let both puddings cool.

When puddings are cooled, add the cocoa to the smaller portion and stir until mixed. Then swirl that mixture into the vanilla pudding after it is poured into the cooked pie shell.

Fay Coppola Natrillo
mother of Angela Harrington
Dominick Gentile Lodge #2332

Ricotta Pie

Filling:

> 3 lbs. ricotta
> 5 whole eggs
> 1 cup sugar
> 1 tsp. vanilla

Crust:

> 3 eggs
> 2 cups flour
> 2 tsp. baking powder
> 1/4 cup sugar
> 1 tsp. vanilla
> 1 stick margarine, melted

Mix the filling ingredients together and set aside.

Mix crust ingredients together and prepare as a regular pie crust, rolled and placed in a 12 inch pie pan.

Pour the filling mixture into the prepared pie crust. Bake at 325 degrees, about 45 minutes. Turn off oven heat. Let the pie stay in the oven until it settles, another 15 to 20 minutes.

Fay Coppola Natrillo
mother of Angela Harrington
Dominick Gentile Lodge #2332

Dolci e Feste: Pies

Wheat Pie

Crust:

2 1/2 cups flour	1 tbsp. baking powder
1/2 stick butter or margarine	3 eggs
1/2 cup sugar	1/2 tsp. vanilla

Wheat preparation:

Almost boil 1 cup of milk and 1 teaspoon sugar (skim wheat), add 1 cup of orange and lemon rinds. Cook for 5 minutes; cool.

Filling:

1/2 lb. wheat, prepared	5 eggs
1 lb. ricotta	salt
1 1/4 cups sugar	orange, vanilla or rum extract

Mix the filling ingredients together. Pour into prepared crust and bake at 325 degrees, approximately 45 to 60 minutes, or until done.

Fay Coppola Natrillo
mother of Angela Harrington
Dominick Gentile Lodge #2332

Dolci e Feste: Pies

Rice Pie

Crust:

2 1/2 cups flour
1/2 stick butter or margarine
1/2 cup sugar
1 tbsp. baking powder
3 eggs
1/2 tsp. vanilla

Mix together for a regular pie crust. Roll out to fit in a 12 inch pie pan.

Filling:

1/2 cup rice, uncooked
1 quart milk
6 eggs, beaten
1 lb. ricotta cheese
1 1/2 cups sugar
1 tbsp. lemon juice, optional
lemon zest, optional

Topping:

confectioners sugar

Cook rice and milk together very slowly until milk is completely absorbed. Sitr occasionally. Remove from heat and let cool. While the rice is cooking, mix together the remaining filling ingredients. Add to the cooled rice mixture and mix together.

Pour into the unbaked pie shell. Bake at 300 degrees for 1 1/2 hours. Change the heat setting to 325 degrees, and bake for another 15 minutes. Sprinkle confectioners sugar on the pie before serving.

Fay Coppola Natrillo
mother of Angela Harrington
Dominick Gentile Lodge #2332

Dolci e Feste

Italian Doughnuts

My mother, Bessie Marinaccio Corozzolo, would make these as a treat.

1 (15 oz.) ricotta cheese
4 eggs
1 tsp. vanilla
1 1/2 cups flour
1/2 tsp. salt

1/2 cup sugar
2 tbsp. baking powder
oil for frying
powdered sugar

Beat cheese with an electric mixer until smooth. Add eggs and vanilla until combined. Add flour, salt, sugar and baking powder. Beat on low speed until just combined. Let dough rest 30 minutes. Drop batter by well rounded teaspoonful, 4 or 5 at a time, into deep fat (365 degrees) for 2 1/2 to 3 minutes until golden brown, turning once. Remove with a slotted spoon and drain on paper towels. Cool completely. Shake doughnuts in a bag with powered sugar or a cinnamon and sugar mixture.

Mary Corozzolo Sorci
John Paul I Lodge #2427

Pizza Dolce I

This delicious dish was always served at Christmas dinner and Easter. However, over the years the family enjoyed it on the Eve with all the other goodies, and left the feast day to the dinner and veggies.

3 lbs. ricotta cheese, whole milk
1 1/2 cups sugar
zest of 2 lemons
1/4 tsp. salt

1 tbsp. vanilla
16 large eggs
3/4 cup cream (optional)

Cream together ricotta and sugar until a very creamy consistency, 5 to 7 minutes (if ricotta is watery, drain to remove excess water). Add lemon, salt, vanilla on low speed. Add eggs, one at a time, mixing very well. Pour mixture into a wax paper-lined 13 x 9 inch pan. Bake at 300 degrees for about 1 1/2 hours. Should a water consistency form on top, blot with paper toweling to remove. Cool in the pan, then cut into small cubes.

Mary DeVito Romano
Mike Accardi Lodge #2441

Dolci e Feste

Pizza Dolce II

3 lbs. whole milk ricotta
12 eggs, beaten
1 cup sugar
1 shot glass of anisette

Blend all ingredients to a creamy consistency. Grease a glass baking dish with butter. Bake at 300 degrees for 1 hour. When golden brown, test the cheesecake with a toothpick. Turn oven off. With the oven door open, leave the cheesecake in the oven to cool.

Maria Mastroserio

Easter Bread with Colored Eggs

1 cup granulated sugar
2 tsp. salt
4 tsp. dried milk solids
1/2 cup all-purpose solid shortening
1/4 cup almond paste
1 1/2 tbsp. corn syrup
3/4 cup eggs (about 3, depending on size)
1/2 cup water
2 tsp. anise
2 tsp. vanilla
3 1/2 to 4 cups flour
2 tbsp. + 1 tsp. baking powder
6 hard boiled colored eggs (must be done in advance)

Add in a mixing bowl the sugar, salt, dried milk solids, shortening, almond paste and corn syrup. Combine and mix well to make a smooth paste. Add eggs, 1 at a time, mixing each well. Add the rest of the liquid ingredients, alternating with dry ingredients. Refrigerate 1 hour. Divide into 6 equal portions. Roll out each portion to 12 inches in length. Braid three together to make 2 loaves. Place loaves on a baking sheet. Brush with egg wash (equal amounts of egg and milk or water, beaten together). Insert 3 eggs into each loaf. Bake in a 350 degree oven until golden brown, about 15 to 20 minutes. Yield: 2 loaves

Ann DeMarco
John Paul I Lodge #2427

Dolci e Feste

Orange Bunnies

5 1/4 to 5 3/4 cups flour
1 pkg. dry yeast
1 1/4 cups milk
1/3 cup sugar
1/2 tsp. salt

1/2 cup butter or margarine
2 eggs
2 tbsp. finely shredded lime peel
1/4 cup orange juice (or 2 tbsp. lime juice and 2 tbsp. water)

In a mixing bowl combine 2 cups flour and yeast, and set aside. In a saucepan heat and stir milk, sugar, and salt just until warm (120 to 130 degrees) and butter until almost melted. Add mixture to dry mixture along with eggs. Beat with mixer for 3 minutes. Using a wooden spoon, stir in orange or lime peel, orange or lime juice, and as much remaining flour as you can. Turn the dough onto a floured surface. Knead in enough flour to make a moderately soft dough that is smooth and elastic. Shape dough into a ball. Place dough in a lightly greased bowl, turn once, cover, and let rise in a warm place until double in size. Punch dough down and form bunnies by cutting strips from the dough and forming a rope between hands, then twist. Pat tips of ears to make a point. Break a piece of dough to form a small ball for the tail. Moisten the ball and place atop dough at bottom of loop, press tail onto dough. After shaping, put onto a greased cookie sheet, cover, and let rise until double (30 to 45 minutes). Bake at 375 degrees for 11 to 12 minutes or until golden brown. Cool on rack.

Orange or Lime Icing: optional

1 1/2 cups confectioners sugar
1 tsp. finely shredded orange or lime peel

2 to 3 tbsp. orange juice (for orange icing)
2 to 3 tbsp. milk (for lime icing)

In a small bowl, combine ingredients based on your icing preference. For orange icing, stir in enough orange juice to make a drizzling consistency. For lime icing, stir in enough milk to make a drizzling consistency.

Ann DeMarco
John Paul I Lodge #2427

Dolci e Feste

Cream Puffs

1/2 quart water
1/2 lb. vegetable shortening
10 oz. all-purpose flour

1 pinch of salt
10 to 12 eggs

Bring water and vegetable shortening to a boil. Simmer, then add the flour and salt. Blend together on low heat for 1 minute.

Place mixture into a large mixing bowl, and using an electric mixer, blend in the eggs, 1 or 2 at a time. Scrape the bowl once or twice while adding eggs. Place batter into a pastry bag.

Line a baking sheet with parchment paper. Shape the dough into small meatball size cream puffs, or larger if desired. For eclairs, shape the dough the size of a ladyfinger. Bake at 400 degrees until golden brown. When cool, fill with the cream of your choice.

Otto Ottaviano
Il Fiore d'Italia Lodge #2811

Scallidy

2 cups wine
5 cups flour
1 tsp. salt

2 tbsp. baking powder
1 cup sugar
oil for frying
honey

Combine first 5 ingredients and mix well. Roll into strips. Cut the strips into 1 inch pieces. Roll over lightly on a grater to make dimples. Deep fry and roll in honey.

Marie M. Colello
John Paul I Lodge #2427

Dolci e Feste

Sfingi

2 eggs
1 lb. ricotta cheese
3 tbsp. sugar

1 cup flour
3 tbsp. baking powder
powdered sugar

Beat eggs, ricotta and sugar. Add flour and baking powder, and mix well. Spoon into hot oil. Cook until golden. Drain. Sprinkle with powdered sugar.

Grace Brooks
Nature Coast Lodge #2502

Zeppole I

1 cup water
1/2 cup margarine
1/8 tsp. salt

1 cup flour
4 eggs

In a saucepan combine water, margarine and salt. Bring to a boil. Add flour all at once, stirring vigorously. Cook, stirring mixture until a ball forms. Remove from heat and cool for about 10 minutes. Add eggs, one at a time, beating after each addition until smooth. Put batter in a pastry tube, with rose tip. On a greased cookie sheet, form a donut shape zeppole. Cook in a 400 degree oven for 30 to 35 minutes or until golden brown. Remove from pan and split, removing any soft dough from inside the zeppole.

Cream custard filling:

  1 pkg. instant vanilla pudding
  1 cup heavy cream

  3/4 cup whole milk
  flavoring (optional)

Fill the zeppole. Sprinkle tops with confectioners sugar, adding a little rose and a piece of cherry on top.

Anne DeMarco
John Paul I Lodge #2427

Dolci e Feste

Zeppole II
Apple and Raisin Fritters

Prepared for the Christmas Eve meal - traditional in Italian homes - can be made without apple or raisins.

1 pkg. dry yeast	4 cups flour
1 tbsp. sugar	1 tsp. salt
1 cup warm water	2 tbsp. oil
1 cup milk	vegetable oil for frying
1/2 cup raisins	honey
1 small apple	

Dissolve yeast and sugar in water. Stir and let stand until foamy. Scald the milk and cool slightly. Soak raisins in warm water. Finely chop 1 small apple. Sift flour into a large bowl. Add salt, oil and liquids. Beat with wooden spoon for 2 minutes. Add apple and drained raisins. Beat 1 minute. Cover with plastic wrap and cloth, and set in a warm place to rise until doubled in bulk, for 1 1/2 hours. Heat at least 2 inches of oil in a 2 or 3 quart saucepan or deep fryer. Spoon batter by tablespoon. Fry until golden brown. Line a colander with paper towels and drain. Serve in a bowl with warmed honey poured over the zeppole.

Anne Ferrone
John Paul I Lodge #2427

Fast Dough

2 1/2 cups flour	1 cup warm water
1 tsp. salt	1 pkg. dry yeast
1 tsp. sugar	

Mix all of the above in a mixer or in a food processor until it forms a stiff dough. Put in a lightly greased bowl and turn the dough. Let dough rise for 45 minutes, or until double in size. *Note:* Can be used for pizza, fried dough or bread.

Ann DeMarco
John Paul I Lodge #2427

Dolci e Feste

Pasta Frolla

1 lb. flour
2 glasses white wine

1/2 cup oil
crisco oil for frying
powdered sugar

Blend the first 3 ingredients, working ingredients to a manageable dough. Roll into a ball and let rest for 20 minutes. Roll out dough to last notch on the pasta machine. Cut into 4 inch strips with a ravioli cutter or straight edge knife. Cut each long strip into 2 inch pieces. Pinch each 4 x 2 inch piece in the middle. Fry in Crisco oil until light golden brown. Dust with powdered sugar or drizzle with honey. *Note:* For a special holiday treat, coat with Vino Cotto (recipe follows).

Vino Cotto

1 grape juice
1 prune juice

1 apple juice
1 lb. brown sugar

Cook slowly until dense and thick, and reduced to one-third, about 4 to 5 hours. Store until needed. Warm cooked vino cotto in a deep fry pan. Dip the fried pasta frolla, one at a time. Store when cooled. Sprinkle with confectioners sugar to serve.

Maria Mastroserio

Dolci e Feste

Castagne in Vino Bianco

When I was a child my grandfather would always do the chestnuts, especially if we had company. My sister and I used to look forward to this delicious dessert.

2 lbs. medium-size chestnuts
3 glasses white wine

1 1/2 cups sugar

Score chestnuts with a cross on the flat side. In a large pan of water, place chestnuts and make sure they are covered with water. Cover pan and cook for about 30 minutes. Drain and peel when cool. Put the wine and sugar in a large, heavy saucepan and heat until it starts to boil. Make certain to stir every 15 minutes over low heat (not boiling). Let cool and serve with ice cream or with a red wine.

Dennis Piasio
Lake Worth/Boynton Beach Lodge #2304

No Bake Rice Pudding

2 cups rice
3/4 cup sugar
1/2 lemon peel, grated
2 cups water
1/2 stick margarine or butter
3/4 gallon milk, regular or lowfat

3 to 4 eggs, beaten
3 cups milk
1/2 to 3/4 tsp. vanilla
1/2 to 3/4 cup sugar
cinnamon

Cook first 5 ingredients until thick, then add 3/4 gallon milk. Over medium heat, stir until rice is cooked. When rice is cooked, mix together with the remaining ingredients, except cinnamon. Bring to a boil. Place in a serving dish. Add cinnamon. Cover and refrigerate until cool.

Anne Cristodero

Dolci e Feste

Sicilian Casateddi

This recipe was given to me by my grandmother, Concetta Pavone. She was born in 1895 and immigrated from Sicily in 1905. As a special treat she would make casateddi at Eastertime, but only with a honey coating. In 1999, I took my first trip to Sicily. Our tour stopped at a coffee shop in the Province of Enna, my grandma's birthplace. There on the display shelf was a platter of casateddi, coated with sugar and cinnamon. Prior to this occasion, I had never come across anyone who was familiar with this delicacy.

Dough:

> 2 cups flour   4 eggs

Sift flour onto a board or counter top, making a well. Break eggs into the well and blend flour into the eggs. Add additional sifted flour if dough sticks to surface. Dough will be stiff. Knead the dough until smooth, adding just enough flour to keep from sticking to the surface. Divide dough into 2 parts and roll out into 2 thin sheets about 1/8 inch thick.

Filling:

> 2 lbs. ricotta   3/4 tsp. cinnamon
> 5 tsp. sugar   vegetable oil for frying

In a bowl mix all of the above ingredients, except oil, with a fork. Place in tablespoon-size mounds on 1 sheet of dough. Cover with second sheet of dough. With fingers, press dough around the mounds, then cut to separate with a sharp knife. Press edges of dough with a fork to seal. The casateddi should look like ravioli. Add 1 inch of vegetable oil to a large skillet. Fry casateddi in medium-high heat until golden brown, turning once. Drain on paper towels. Coat with one of the following recipes:

Honey coating: 1 cup honey

Heat the honey over low heat until it becomes thin. Dip fried casateddi into the honey on both sides. Place on a serving plate. Serve warm or at room temperature.

Dolci e Feste

Sugar coating: 1 cup granulated sugar
1/2 tsp. cinnamon

Mix sugar with cinnamon in a dish. Dip hot casateddi into sugar mix on both sides. Place on a serving plate. Serve warm or at room temperature.

Marie Sommovigo
Dominick Gentile Lodge #2332

Zeppole di San Giuseppe
St. Joseph's Day Cream Puffs

Batter:

1 cup hot water
1/2 cup butter
1 tbsp. sugar

1 pinch of salt
1 cup flour, added all at once

Bring to a boil in a saucepan the above ingredients. Beat with a wooden spoon until mixture leaves sides of pan and forms a smooth ball (about 5 minutes). Remove from heat. Quickly beat in 4 eggs (one at a time) beating until smooth after each addition. Continue beating until mixture is smooth and glossy. Add 1 teaspoon grated orange peel and 1 teaspoon grated lemon peel. Mix thoroughly. Drop by tablespoons 2 inches apart on a greased baking sheet. Bake at 450 degrees 15 to 20 minutes. Remove to a rack to cool completely. Cut a slit in the side of each puff and fill with ricotta filling.

Ricotta filling:

1 1/2 lbs. ricotta cheese
1 tbsp. grated orange rind
2 tbsp. grated lemon rind
1/4 cup flour

1 tbsp. vanilla
1 pinch of salt
4 eggs
1 cup sugar

Combine the filling ingredients, except eggs and sugar. In a separate bowl, beat eggs until foamy; add sugar gradually, beating until eggs are thick. Stir beaten eggs into ricotta mixture until well blended and smooth. Fill puffs.

Joseph B. Franzalia Lodge #2422

Dolci e Feste

Cenci per il Berlingaccio
Shrove Tuesday Sweet Knots

This is a Shrove Tuesday tradition in Tuscany.

2 cups flour
1/3 cup sugar
1 tsp. baking powder
1/4 tsp. salt
2 eggs
2 tbsp. butter, softened
2 tbsp. brandy
oil for deep frying
confectioners sugar or
1 pint whipping cream

Sift flour, sugar, baking powder and salt on a pastry board. Make a depression in the center and add eggs, butter and brandy. Beat with a fork until most of the flour is absorbed. Mix with hands and knead into a smooth paste or soft dough. Wrap the dough in wax paper and refrigerate for 1 hour. Roll thin on a floured board. Cut into strips 1 1/2 x 5 inches. Tie into a knot and deep fry over medium heat, a few at a time, until golden brown and puffed. Sprinkle with confectioners sugar or whipped cream. Yield: 6 to 8 servings

Margaret Scarfia
John Paul I Lodge #2427

Struffoli
Honey Balls - Quick and Easy

1 cup sugar
6 tbsp. oil
3 eggs
4 cups flour
1 1/2 tbsp. baking powder
1/2 tsp. salt
2 tbsp. vanilla
oil for frying
honey
almonds
candy sprinkles

Using an electric mixer, mix together the sugar, oil and eggs. Add the flour, then the baking powder, salt and vanilla. Mix until it starts to form a dough. Place on a board and knead until it forms a soft dough. Cut into pieces and roll to form a rope. Cut rope into desired size pieces. Deep fry until light brown. Put on brown paper to cool, then put in a large bowl. Heat honey and add to the struffoli. Mix well. Mound the struffoli on a dish and add almonds and candy sprinkles.

Pauline Nicolosi
Delray Beach Lodge #2719

Dolci e Feste

Stuffed Dates

1 lb. dates
1 lb. pecan halves
1/4 cup margarine
3/4 cup light brown sugar
1 egg

1 1/4 cups flour
1/2 cup sour cream
1 tsp. baking soda
1/2 tsp. baking powder
1/4 tsp. salt

Mix the last 8 ingredients to make a dough. Stuff dates with the pecan halves. Cover each date with some of the dough. Bake in a 350 degree oven for 8 to 10 minutes. Mix the frosting ingredients together, and use to frost the stuffed dates.

Frosting:

1/2 cup margarine, melted
3/4 cup powdered sugar

3/4 tsp. vanilla
milk, as needed

Mary Lou Pagonico
Township Lodge #2624

Torrone

Add (use any ratio of 2 nuts to 1 sugar)

3 cups almonds
1 1/2 cups sugar

Spray a cookie sheet lightly. Mix ingredients and heat on high in a cast iron or heavy aluminum fry pan, stirring constantly until sugar starts to melt. Reduce heat to medium or low, stirring constantly until all sugar has melted. Boil slightly. Nuts should be nice and brown but not burned. Pour onto a prepared cookie sheet and spread out as thick as you want. Let cool completely. Break into pieces and put in glass jars only. It will stick together if you do not put it in glass.

Pauline Nicolosi
Delray Beach Lodge #2719

Dolci e Feste

Fried Ravioli

This was a traditional dessert at Christmas, along with the cucciddata. Thank you, Grandma Dimitri and Aunt Millie, for all of these wonderful memories.

3 lbs. flour	3/4 lb. Crisco, room temperature
2 cups sugar	warm water for mixing
1 tsp. salt	

Mix the above ingredients and knead dough until smooth. Cut the dough in half and roll out both pieces with a rolling pin. Set aside.

Filling:

2 lbs. ricotta, drained	1/2 cup chocolate chips, chopped
2 cups sugar	2 cups citrus fruit, chopped

Mix the above filling ingredients together. Take one piece of the rolled dough, and cut out circles using the rim of a glass or a round cookie cutter. Drop a full tablespoon of filling in the center of each circle.

Take the second piece of rolled out dough, cut out more circles, then place the second set of circles over the ones with the filling. Pinch the ends all around with a fork to seal, and using a toothpick, make a small hole on the top of each ravioli.

Pour any type oil in a large frying pan; fry the ravioli on both sides until golden brown. While the ravioli are still warm, sprinkle them with a mixture of brown sugar and cinnamon. Serve warm.

Carole Cositore
Societa d'Italia Lodge #2698

Dolci e Feste

Pizza Rustica di Bari
(at Eastertime)

1/2 lb. each:
  mortadella, diced
  prosciutto cotto, diced
  soppressata, diced
  provolone, diced
  mozzarella, diced

8 eggs, beaten
1/2 cup grated parmesan cheese

Blend all ingredients. Pour into a baking dish lined with Pasta Frolla. Cover dish with rolled out Pasta Frolla. Trim edges and pinch top and bottom layer together to form a seal. Snip top of dish with scissors making 4 to 6 cuts to let steam escape when cooking. Bake at 400 degrees for 25 to 30 minutes.

Sanquinaccio Renza

3/4 lb. cooked pork blood, finely chopped
flour
3 tbsp. sugar
2 cups milk
3 egg yolks

1/2 tsp. vanilla
1/4 cup butter
2 squares baking chocolate
1 tbsp. pine nuts
2 tbsp. diced candied fruits
mint leaf, optional

Purchase cooked blood in an Italian butcher shop. Mix flour, sugar, milk, egg yolks and vanilla. Cook in a saucepan over low heat, stirring steadily until consistency is smooth and creamy. Add butter and very finely chopped blood to the creamy mixture and strain. Melt the chocolate squares and mix with nuts and fruits. Place in the refrigerator for 2 to 4 hours. Serve nice and cold. Garnish with a mint leaf.

Eleanor Renza
Delray Beach Lodge #2719

Dolci e Feste

Grandpa Cuzzie's Struffoli

Grandma Cositore always made the struffoli for Christmas. I remember the hope chest in her bedroom topped with bowls and bowls of these tasty honey balls. What a treat for dessert during the Christmas season! Years after Grandma died, my father Cuzzie and my mom Gilda decided to make the struffoli for Christmas. My dad, never having seen my Grandmother make these honey balls (or didn't remember), thought after cutting the long logs into pieces that he then had to hand-roll each piece of dough. Can you imagine how long it took mom and dad to get the dough ready for frying? Every year when I make struffoli, I remember how we all laughed when dad told us his story. How I miss him and his crazy sense of humor...I wish I could tease him today about rolling the honey balls.

1 lb. flour
6 eggs
1 1/2 tsp. vanilla

1 1/2 tsp. baking powder
pinch of salt
cooking oil

Place flour in a mound and make a well in the center. Add eggs one at a time, mixing slightly after each addition. Add remaining ingredients and mix thoroughly. Turn dough on to a lightly floured surface and knead. Cover dough with a damp towel; let rest for 1 hour at room temperature. Keeping most of the dough under the towel to prevent its drying, tear off a small piece with your fingers and roll it between your hands into a 1/2-inch thick log. Cut log into 1/2-inch pieces. Repeat process until all dough has been cut and shaped.
Heat oil in a deep fry pan. Fry dough in batches until golden brown. Remove from oil with a slotted spoon and transfer to paper towels to drain.

Honey Mixture:
1 cup honey
1/2 cup sugar

dash of lemon juice
2 tbsp. water

Add all ingredients to a large pot and bring to a boil. Lower heat to simmer and cook until foam disappears, approximately 5 minutes. Coat a wooden spoon with cooking spray; remove pan from heat and add balls a few at a time, stirring well with prepared spoon. Transfer honey balls to a dish and sprinkle with colored sprinkles. If desired, stir again to cover the honey balls completely.

Marie Bosco
Sister of Grand Lodge of Florida President Dan Cositore
Societa D'Italia #2698

Index

Palm Bay Lodge 2823
Palm Bay

Daughters of Italy Lodge 2825
Clearwater

Highlands County Lodge 2830
Sebring

Buona Fortuna Lodge 2835
Pensacola

Polk County Lodge 2836
Winter Haven

Fort Myers Lodge 2839
Fort Myers

Index

Antipasti / Appetizers

Acciuga Imbattite di Memy 20
Antipasto 10
Artichoke Dip 9
Artichoke Hearts 9
Bagno Caldo alla Siciliana 11
BLT Bites 12
Bruschetta with Tomatoes 12
Bruschetta 11
Cheesy Italian Bread 13
Clam Dip 14
Crocchette 13
Croquettes 13
Crusty Italian Sausage Bites 14
Eggplant Sandwiches 15
Fiori di Zucchini Fritti 17
Fried Zucchini Flowers 17
Garlic Crostini 9
Grilled Warm Antipasto 16
Hot Dip Italian Style 11
Insalata con Olive 15
Lumache Marchigiana 16
Mozzarella Croquettes 18
Mushrooms in Vinegar 18
Olive Salad 15
Pepperoni Stuffed Mushrooms 17
Ricotta and Tomato Bruschetta 19
Sausage Cheese Balls 18
Stuffed Anchovy Appetizer 21
Tomatoes, Mozzarella, Anchovy and Black Olives 19
Tuna with Onion 20
Zucchini Pie 21
Zucchini Quiche 20

Minestre / Soups

Beef Soup 25
Bread Soup 32
Bronx Home Run Zucchini Soup 26
Brown Rice and Lentil Soup 26
Ceci Soup 27
Chicken Soup 27
Chicken Soup 28
Cioppino 29
Egg & Parmesan Strands in Broth 33
Escarole Soup 36
Escarole, Bean and Sausage Soup 29
Joey's White Bean and Sausage Soup 30
Mediterranean Chickpea, Tomato and Pasta Soup 31
Mushroom Soup 31
Panara 32
Passatelli 33
Pasta e Fagioli 34
Potato Soup 34
Spinach and Meatball Soup 35
Tortellini Soup 35
Zuppa di Pollo 27
Zuppa di Escarole 36

Pane e Pizze / Bread

Cinnamon Bread Ring (for Bread Machine) 41
Easy Sausage Bread 42
Fried Dough 45
Garlic Bread 45
Italian Bread Ring 43
Olive and Oregano Bread 44
Pane alle Olive ed Origano 44
Pepper Rolls 43
Pizza Fritta 45

Sausage Bread 42

Le Uova / Eggs

Fritatta Primavera 49
Frittata Di Funghi 49
Mushroom Omelet 49
My Sister's Omelette 50
Omelette 50
Scrambled Eggs and Pepperoni 51
Spaghetti Frittata 51
Sunday Morning Eggs 50

Salsa-Pasta-Riso-Polenta

Angel Hair Pasta with Chicken 59
Arugula Marinara Sauce 55
Baked Gnocchi 60
Bigole 55
Bolognese Sauce 56
Cannelloni 65
Capellini with Sausage and Spinach 61
Due Fettuccine con Prosciutto 62
Gnocchi 59
Fettuccine with Prosciutto 59
Golden Onion Orzo 66
Grandma Marietta's Ravioli 81
Italian Rice Balls 76
Linguine with Vodka Sauce 70
Manicotti 72
Marinara Sauce 57
Mom's Favorite Spaghetti Pie 63
Orzo with Vegetables 66
Pasta and Arugula 60
Pasta and Ceci 63
Pasta and Fava Beans 70

Pasta Napoli	61
Pasta Rustica	73
Polenta Filled Manicotti	64
Ragu Bolognese alla Rocchina's Mama	56
Ravioli Napoletan	68
Ravioli with Stuffing	67
Rice and Mushrooms Country Style	78
Rice Balls I	77
Rice Balls II	77
Rice Balls III	78
Rigatoni with Cinnamon Beef	68
Rigatoni with Onion Sauce	62
Risi e Bisi	79
Risotto con Funghi alla Contadina	78
Risotto	79
Salsa di Noci	57
Sausage Bow Tie Pasta	69
Soft Polenta	80
Spaghetti and Asparagus	74
Spaghetti and Chicken Livers	75
Spaghetti con Fegatini di Pollo	75
Spaghetti with Meatballs	71
Spinach and Pasta	73
Stephanie's Broccoli Rabe and Sausage over Pasta	75
Summer Pasta Sauce	58
Tortellini with Scallops alla Michael	69
Vegetable Pasta Sauce	58

Carne-Pollo-Pesce / Meat-Chicken-Fish

Acciughe Marinate Napoletana	112
Anguilla I	112
Anguilla II	113
Baked Eel	112
Baked Fish Oregano	123
Baked Sardines	126

Baked Stuffed Squid	117
Beef Steak and Bell Peppers	86
Bistecca ai Peperoni	86
Bistecca alla Pizzaiola	85
Braciola	87
Braised Turkey Wings	104
Buridda Genovese	114
Calamari con Pomodoro	114
Calamari Imbottiti	115
Calamari Ripieni al Forno	117
Calamari Ripieni	116
Calamari Salad	118
Cappuzelle	100
Chicken and Sausage Scarpariello	108
Chicken alla Ischia	105
Chicken Cacciatore	106
Chicken Fra Diavolo	104
Chicken Francese	110
Chicken in Sauce	108
Chicken Piccata	106
Chicken with Artichokes	105
Chicken with Prosciutto & Tomatoes over Polenta	107
Chicken with Sun-Dried Tomatoes & Artichokes	109
Clam Cakes	118
Clams Casino	119
Clams Crostini	119
Coniglio	101
Coteghino and Lentils	94
Cotolette di Agnello	99
Crab Mariner's Style	120
Delicious Tongue Dinner	102
Family Style Oxtail	101
Fish Salad – Three Fishes	130
Fish with Tomato Sauce	113
Fried Eel	113
Garmugia	86

Geri's Meatballs	88
Granchi Marinara	120
Grilled Beef Hearts	89
Grilled Butterfish	130
Grilled Calamari	116
Insalata di Gamberi	122
Italian Sausage Casserole	93
Lamb Sweetbreads with Prosciutto	99
Lamb's Brains	100
Mama's Beef and Peppers	87
Marinated Raw Anchovies	112
Marinated Shrimp	121
Mullet with Prosciutto	122
Mussels Marinara	126
My Grandfather's Saltimbocca	95
Our Family Style Tripe	102
Peppers and Sausage Napoletan Style	91
Pesce Oreganata	123
Pesce Spado a Gliotta	124
Pheasant with Cream	109
Pollo alla Bolognese	111
Porgy with Peas	123
Quick Skillet Crab Cover	120
Rabbit Country-Style	101
Rice with Mussels, Carrots and Peas	125
Roast Beef Scalzitti	89
Rolled Beef Roman Style	90
Saltimbocca	96
Sardines with Tomato Sauce	127
Sausage with Rapini	93
Sautéed Seafood and Veggies	128
Scungilli Chowder	127
Seafood alla Corsetti	128
Seafood and Eggplant Casserole	129
Shrimp Salad	122
Shrimp with Arugula Sauce	121
Sicilian Meat Roll	90
Spetine: Beef Rolls	92

Spiedini I 91
Spiedini II 92
Squid with Tomatoes 114
Steamed Cod 128
Stewed Tripe: Grandma's Recipe 103
Sticky Garlic Skewers 110
Stufato di Trippa 103
Stuffed Squid 115
Swordfish Messina Style 124
Turf and Surf Stew Tuscan Style 94
Veal Florentine 96
Veal Marsala with Artichoke Hearts 97
Veal Marsala 97
Veal Stew 98
White Clam Sauce 129

Insalate e Contorni / Salads & Vegetables

Artichoke and Chickpea Salad 137
Artichoke and Green Bean Romano 135
Artichokes, Prosciutto and Parmigiana 135
Asparagi alla Parmigiana 136
Asparagus with Parmigiana 136
Baked Cauliflower 142
Baked Zucchini Gratin 155
Bean Salad 138
Boiled Celery and Chickpeas 139
Broccoli Rabe with Mushrooms 141
Broccoli Rabe with Sausage 141
Butter Bean Sauté 138
Cauliflower Sheriff's Style 143
Cavolfiore al Forno 142
Cavolfiore alla Scheriffo 143
Cavolfiore Fritto 142
Condimento per Insalata 156
Egg, Orange and Sweet Potato Salad 151
Eggplant and Polenta Parmigiana 145
Eggplant Lasagna 145

Eggplant Parmigiana 147
Eggplant, Prosciutto and Mozzarella Rollups 146
Escarola Imbottita 149
Escarole Parmesan 150
Finocchio alla Genovese 147
Fried Cauliflower 142
Gorgonzola Salad Dressing 156
Grilled Eggplant 144
Insalata con Olive 150
Insalata di Fagiolini 139
Insalata di Uova, Arancia e Patate 151
Marinated Eggplant 146
Olive Salad 150
Potato Cake 151
Red Bean Salad 140
Roasted Eggplant and Bell Pepper Sandwiches 148
Salad Dressing 156
Sedano e Ceci Stufato 139
Spinach Cheese Bake 152
String Bean Salad 139
Stuffed Artichokes I 136
Stuffed Artichokes II 137
Stuffed Eggplant 144
Stuffed Escarole Leaves 149
Stuffed Peppers 152
Tortelloni Salad 153
Vascotti and Beans 140
Zucchini Frittata 154
Zucchini Pie 154
Zucchini Sausage Pie 153

Dolci e Le Sante Feste / Desserts & Holidays

Almond Cookies 162
Apple Pie 187
Aunt Millie's Anise Cookies 163
Biscotti Abbruzzese 161
Cannoli Cake 182

Castagne in Vino Bianco 201
Cenci per il Berlingaccio 204
Cheesecake a la Chiyoko 178
Cheese-Raisin Pound Cake 181
Cherry Slices 164
Chiyoko's Tomato Soup Cake 180
Cranberry Pistachio Biscotti 161
Cream Puffs 197
Crumb Cake Supreme 181
Cuccidati 166
Durdilla 171
Easter Bread with Colored Eggs 195
Easter Rice Pie 189
Easter Ricotta Pie 188
Easy Ricotta Marble Cake 185
Egg Biscuits 164
Fast Dough 199
Fig Bars 166
Fried Ravioli 206
Funzis Cookies 163
Grandpa Cuzzie's Struffoli 208
Honey Balls – Quick and Easy 204
Italian Cheesecake 179
Italian Christmas Wine Cookie 171
Italian Cream Pie 190
Italian Doughnuts 194
Italian Fig Bars 167
Italian Honey Cookies 175
Italian Molasses Cookies 169
Italian Rice Cake 183
Italian Rum Cake 186
Lemon Drop Cookies 168
Mama Sacco's Biscotti 165
Mostaccioli 172
Nana's Pastry 170
No Bake Rice Pudding 201
One Step Pound Cake 184
Orange Bunnies 196

Pasta Frolla	200
Peach Ricotta Pie	187
Pepper Biscuits	170
Pignoli Cookies	173
Pineapple Cookies	169
Pistachio Biscotti	162
Pizza Dolce I	194
Pizza Dolce II	195
Pizza Rustica di Bari	207
Pizzelle	172
Quick Cheesecake	179
Rice Pie	193
Ricotta Cheesecake	180
Ricotta Pie	191
Sanquinaccio Renza	207
Scallidy	197
Sesame Cookies	174
Sfinge	198
Shrove Tuesday Sweet Knots	204
Sicilian Casateddi	202
Spumoni Cake	185
St. Joseph's Day Cream Puffs	203
Struffoli	204
Stuffed Dates	205
Thumbprint Cookies	174
Tordilli	175
Torrone	205
Vino Cotto	200
Wheat Pie	192
Wine Biscuits I	176
Wine Biscuits II	176
Zeppole di San Giuseppe	203
Zeppole I	198
Zeppole II	199
Zuppa Inglese	186